Preserving Light

Preserving Light

Gail Hartman

Olive Press
Minneapolis, Minnesota

As far as we can discern, the sole purpose of human existence is to kindle a light in the darkness of mere being.

~ Carl Jung

Let everything happen to you: beauty and terror. Just keep going. No feeling is final.

~ Rainer Maria Rilke

ISBN: 978-1-7333247-2-4

Library of Congress Control Number: 9781733324724

Published by

Olive Press

Minneapolis, Minnesota

CONTENTS

Introduction

❧

Introduction

I surprised myself the morning I called the tarot card reader. I had gotten her name from a patient, who had consulted her due to a complex and seemingly irresolvable dilemma concerning her adult son. The patient and I worked together tirelessly for months and then she took a vacation with her husband. When she returned, she was buoyant in a way I had never experienced her. She told me how she had transformed the predicament with her son — and there was a tarot card reader involved in the explanation. I was humbled. So much for all my training as a psychotherapist, my Jungian and psychoanalytic studies. I was less helpful than a tarot card reader. So of course, I copied down her name and number.

It was about eight weeks after Peter died, a Sunday. I was carrying the weight of early grief and was wandering around my house, going through piles of condolence cards and forcing myself to clean out his dresser drawers. I paced myself well, as I remember, and collapsed when I needed to wherever I was in the house. On this particular Sunday, I took a break from the sad details of loss and sat at my desk, overwhelmed. I opened my 2012 planner and the index card on which I had written the tarot card reader's name and number fell out of it. The synchronicity, the timing were not lost on me. So I picked up the phone and called her.

Amazingly, she answered. We spoke for only a few minutes and set up a time during the following week for a session. She asked me to be thinking of what I wanted to know from the cards, to write down three or four questions. She explained that she had been studying the tarot for 25 years. She sounded very sane, no New Age hocus-pocus. Her name was not Venus Dreamcatcher or Crystal Morning Star, but simply Therese Stanton.

My questions in hand, I called Therese at the scheduled time. She likes to do readings by phone, even though she lives in Minneapolis; she does not want to be influenced by body language. This seemed smart, and I was happy to be in the comfort of my own home for this appointment.

I told her that my husband, Peter, had recently died and my questions had to do with his life, his death and how I was going to survive this tremendous loss. She used four decks during this two-and-a-half-hour reading. I was bowled over by her insight and her wisdom. She seemed to be aware of things she could not possibly have known. It was one of the most remarkable conversations I had ever had.

Here are the most salient points she made that relate to this book of my writing:

1. Peter, while he died way too young, had completed what he was put on the earth to do (which seemed totally correct to me).

2. It was all over the decks of cards that I had not yet done what I was born to do (which caused me to stop breathing for a moment).

3. It was imperative that I take this seriously and devote the time and energy to being in sync with what my being and soul have wanted to do for my entire life.

4. It would be necessary for me to either quit my job or at least cut back dramatically in order to make time for this most important endeavor.

5. She asked me if I knew what this was, this something I had not yet done. I said, *Yes, I think I do.* I was shaking.

6. She asked me just to concentrate on what I knew this to be and then she laid out the cards, saying the following: *Oh my God, Gail, you have to hear this.* I said, *I'm listening.* And she said, *No I really, really mean it. You must listen to this.* And I repeated, *I'm listening.* I started to cry

because I knew what she was going to say. All four decks came up with the same message: *You must write. You are a writer and you are not writing. It is critical that you write.*

I cried tears of recognition and relief. To hear someone so forcefully state what I have known from the time I was 15 was astounding. I had been paralyzed in this area, so neurotically stalled. I used to say to Peter that I was stuck on the tip of my own tongue. I had even gone into therapy a time or two to talk about this problem of wanting to write, yet not being able to make myself do it. I learned all kinds of possible explanations for my dilemma. My mother was an editor of many well-known writers for a publishing company in New York City during my entire childhood. She had wanted to be a writer herself, but instead spent her life editing other people's writing. Some of the voices in my head: *Who do you think you are wanting to be a writer? If your mother couldn't do it, then how can you do it? No one will be interested in what you write, so don't bother. You've wasted all this time not writing, so how can you start now?* You get the picture. Deadly messages.

So here I was, in the throes of grief, talking to a stranger on the phone, weeping about what I have always known to be true. I decided to take this to heart. It was only two months from Peter's death when I realized he was dead, but I was not. I was alive and needed to take my life seriously — which meant I needed to write as though it actually mattered.

I began writing poetry soon after that tarot session; the poems were mostly about love, loss and grief. Yet, I kept stalling out. I would pick myself up and eke out another verse, but I was dribbling, sputtering, not fully behind myself. I had become close friends with Kate Tucker, a newly retired Unitarian Universalist minister who had officiated at the memorial service for Peter. She and I often talked about writing and creativity, hoping to light a spark in one another. One summer day, she was having tea with Ann Reed at Turtle Bread in the Longfellow neighborhood of Minneapolis. They came up with an idea to meet on a regular basis and to encourage each other to stay loyal to their wishes to be creative. They decided to call me and invite me to join them. I was just getting to know Ann personally. I had greatly admired her and her music from afar for years and years. She could not possibly be conflicted about writing, I thought. But yes, she also grappled with the isolation of being a creative person and was eager to see if convening regularly would help us be more generative.

The first time we met, we told one another about our struggles with writing and being congruent with our wishes to create. I told Kate and Ann that I had been suffering off and on in my life regarding this rut I had settled into as a second home of sorts, often wondering if a part of me was dying. I knew I needed to write; it was embedded inside me somewhere, an essential part of my soul and I was not honoring it, which made me profoundly sad and, at times, frightened.

I think this must have resonated inside Ann, because starting the next day, she texted me the following: *Did you write anything today?* And I replied, *No. Sadly, no.* And the next day, she texted me: *Are you putting aside any time for a bit of writing today?* And this continued for weeks and weeks. She nudged me into facing my self. Finally the rubber met the road and I began to write. I am deeply indebted to Ann for her persistence and belief in me as a writer, and to Kate for her constant encouragement and support and for introducing me to Ann so that the three of us could form what has been a creative lifeline.

Now it is almost seven years later. Therese was right. I have changed my work schedule radically to allow me the time to write. I took what I called a sabbatical from my psychotherapy practice (a patient called it my "maternity leave") in the summer of 2016. I wrote for seven weeks straight. I never left town. And then I decided that I would have to start seeing fewer patients, and so I have cut my practice in half. I still love my work, but as I enter my 70s, I am acutely aware that if I don't spend the time doing what I was put on the earth to do, I might die unhappy and unfulfilled. Aging is a gift in some ways. It sharpens our inner eyesight. It helps us separate the essential from the extraneous. It is a big green light that is screaming out: *Go! Get out there! If you don't, it may be too late.*

This book is a compilation of my writing over the last two years, with a few pieces inserted from the past. It was Ann's thoughtful suggestion that I create it as gift to myself for this milestone birthday. It is evidence that I miraculously turned a corner; I became unstuck. I never thought this could happen. And it has. Three women led me to this: Therese, Kate and Ann. My gratitude to them is immeasurable.

Poetry

Preserving Light
(November 10, 2016)

This year
I will preserve light.
Jars once filled with
jams and jellies,
pickles and peaches,
summer tomatoes
will be used instead
to bottle
the radiance of autumn.
My jars will be chalices of light:
silky yellow gray of early dawn,
illuminated noontimes,
brilliant sun against
a sapphire sky,
hazy glow at dusk,
the white light
of the moon.

I will attach labels:
Golden
Luminous
Fading
Late-Lingering
Warm-Western
Diffuse.

Like heirloom tomatoes
preserved for winter,
I will can light.
I will reach for a jar
in the days of darkness.
I will reach for a jar
when the world is unknowable.

I will reach for a jar
on an inconceivable January day
when light is dimmed by gloom.
I will reach for a jar as a reminder:
behind dark shadows
light slithers through.
It reappears without fail in the spring,
that revolution around the sun;
that revolution, our revolution,
from darkness into light.

Homage to the Pilot

Last night
I'm sure you did
what I did
and what all the passengers did
which was to eat dinner
chew the vegetables
drink the water
(not wine, we hope)
and then finish with dessert.
Perhaps you decided
to shave before bed:
so much to get ready
in the early morning
when the alarm rings and rings
and you are up
springing out of bed
toward the blue uniform
with red epaulets
like an avian specimen
on someone's bird list.

You drive to the airport
parking next to other red-winged
manbirds
and walk to the terminal
which, by the way,
should not be called a terminal
if you give it a little thought,
and you proceed,
as do the passengers,
toward the shiny 757.
And though we stand in different lines

and we board at different times
we are all together
intending to leave here and go there.

We, the passengers, know
you are God for the next few hours:
so thank you for learning about turbulence
and aerodynamics and
thank you for not drinking wine last night and
for paying constant attention
to all the dials and meters
and also for remembering
that each one of us,
like you, I'm sure,
loves a child or a mother
and perhaps this love is complicated,
not smooth at this very moment
so we might really really need
to land and meet this person
to straighten out misunderstandings.
Not everyone has their affairs in order
at 35,000 feet.

So please know that we
at the rear of the plane
send you our love and gratitude
for finishing high school and college
and for getting any rebellious parts
of yourself worked out
so that you can somehow,
through some miraculous maneuvers,
get this 250,000-pound

silver projectile we are in
to lightly meet the ground
so that all of us,
you too, I'm sure,
can look forward to continuing
this beautiful life.

Pomp and Circumstance

The sports arena,
red roses for sale in the lobby:
gifts for graduates.
Families flow in,
small children awestruck,
babies squirming,
grandparents beaming pride,
glad to be alive,
their child's child
filing into rows of chairs,
where only a week ago
a boy, as tall as a giraffe,
sank a three-pointer
and cheerleaders,
athletic jumping beans
in ponytails,
squealed their zeal
to season ticket holders.

A procession rehearsed
the day before,
the graduates parade in,
cloaked in black
like penguins with caps
topped with cardboard squares,
golden tassels
dancing in their eyes,
they walk
single-file
from the locker rooms
onto center court.

The school band,
under the scoreboard,
begins playing:
Pomp and Circumstance,
the tune for this transition,
the saddest happy song.

We witness them one by one,
not children, but grown,
not skilled, but educated,
smiles concealing their fears.
They wave to the crowd
as though returning
from a tour of duty
in one piece,
still standing.

The future starts
when the music stops.
Unsure, but hopeful,
they step out into the sun,
into the arms
of someone who believes in them,
someone who cannot
do more than they have done,
who tells them to go,
go and make your mark.
They pose for pictures, arms entwined,
parents letting go, holding on.
The end is as much the beginning
as the beginning is the end.

Ambiguity in the air,
they wave these new diplomas,
their names in elegant calligraphy
cascading all over the world.

What We Memorize

Twelve inches in a foot and three feet in a yard
and, of course, E equals mc squared;
the months in a year,
the oceans and Great Lakes,
the planets and sometimes their order.
A penny saved is a penny earned
and rolling stones gather no moss.
i before *e* except after *c*,
ZIP codes, passwords and, of course,
a through *z*.
Absence makes the heart grow fonder
unless out of sight is out of mind.
Whose woods these are I think I know ...
but they are not in Jackson or Juneau,
Boise or Charleston,
nor any state capitals
we know by rote.
We the people of the United States ...
go to market, to market to buy a fat pig ...
while reciting *hey, diddle, diddle*
and riddles galore.
Show me the way to go home with
the map engraved in my brain
alongside *Four score and seven years ago ...*
We row, row, row our boats gently down the Mississippi,
spelling it forward and backward
as we try not to step on cracks
to save our mothers' backs,
and to keep our bones from sticks and stones
we learn poems by heart,
because words will never hurt us.

My Résumé, a prose poem

1. I was born in a city of 8 million people called New York. It was crowded and vertical. My hometown newspaper was the *New York Times*.

2. In the year of my birth, the State of Israel was created. Ronald Reagan divorced his first wife, Jane Wyman. Gandhi was assassinated in New Delhi. Alfred Kinsey issued a revolutionary report on *Sexual Behavior in the Human Male*. Tennessee Williams won a Pulitzer Prize for *A Streetcar Named Desire*. Babe Ruth died, as did Orville Wright. And a first-class postage stamp cost 3 cents.

3. My parents stayed very busy making their mark. My mother saw to it that some good books were published. My father made house calls and paid attention to the hearts of other people.

4. I went to a small all-girls school. I was 18 the first time I met a boy. To tell you the truth, it was anti-climactic, but still pleasant.

5. I made a four-year calendar by hand when I was 14, so that I could mark off the days one by one, until I could get out of the city. While my younger sister loved New York, I hated its loneliness, its crowds, its prohibitions: don't touch, don't talk to strangers, don't cross the street. Danger was lurking everywhere. And 9/11 was 40 years away.

6. I learned some important things in New York: money and happiness have no relationship with one another; ethnocentrism can be a form of prejudice; and psychotherapy is the greatest way to journey inward.

7. I escaped finally to a college in Ohio. This was farther west than anyone in my family had ever gone. My parents feared for me.

8. I loved Ohio. I loved how green it was and how the houses had roofs like triangles, not the flat-line ones of New York. I loved the passion of the antiwar demonstrators. I learned I was a part of an incredible generation. I belonged somewhere.

9. In college, I learned about art history, French literature, creative writing and sex.

10. I moved to our nation's capital for a year, married to a nice man. We had two nice cats. I worked at a magazine called *National Geographic* and I was miserable. I hated the East Coast. I had to get out. Again.

11. We moved to North Dakota, which I know sounds dramatic. It was. My parents almost called the police. There are so many ways to rebel.

12. I fell in love with North Dakota: the flat mustard fields, the summer swimming holes, the adventure of living in a place that was totally foreign to me. I had never heard of the places I discovered: Minot, Manvel, Devils Lake, Durbin, Bisbee, Buxton. The map was like a poem.

13. My marriage was not like a poem, so it ended. He moved to the East Coast and I stayed for six more winters, to be exact. In those years, I found myself. A girl from Manhattan finds out who she is in Grand Forks, North Dakota. Almost a tabloid headline.

14. But just listen to the wealth I acquired in North Dakota: I became a potter; I taught braille; I collected stamps (but only pretty ones); I planted vegetables; I discovered, while driving due south to Fargo at dawn, that the sun rises in the east and sets in the west — which we had only heard about in New York. I studied psychology. I also met and married the love of my life.

15. He and I left North Dakota and moved next door to Minnesota. Years and years of making a household or two, making a baby or two, raising these babies, working at jobs I have loved: at a bookstore, at a radio station, and finally practicing psychotherapy.

16. Illness came into our Minnesota house, but then recovery, for a time, did, too. We learned to replace fear with hope, although I never got very good at it. When I drive by a hospital now, I look up and wish all the patients freedom from pain and waiting.

17. In New York, my father died at some point. A bittersweet loss. We spread his ashes in the Atlantic Ocean. My mother knew he hated sand, but oh well.

18. The children left home. I cried for years. I missed my son as though something in my soul had been amputated. But now I have become accustomed to the quiet. New York is very far away. I almost never go there. I prefer this place, with its magical storms, its grain elevators downtown, its lakes and even its limitations, none of which I can think of at the moment.

19. Not much time left for me: with good luck, 20 more winters and 20 more gardens. At the beginning, they don't tell you what matters most: one beautiful ordinary day after another in a place you feel is home.

Restraint

I rein myself in:
underexpressed, considered
and responsible,
knowing not everything need be uttered.

Full disclosure
is for the courtroom,
I tell myself,
and for rituals of confession.

I curb my endearments,
I shelve my deepest passions
as I show restraint,
another way of loving.

Flow

What interrupts it is sludge,
outlawed feelings, suppressed

forbidden longings, stockpiled
in a tender heart.

Too much restraint is a bad thing,
I tell myself

and am left with the dilemma:
how do I stay fluid

like the stream that moves
so easily over rocks, fallen trees,

through beaver dams
and cattail thickets,

forming rapids, glistening like satin,
babbling its song;

the sound makes you thirsty
as you pine for thick forest,

the deep dark region
where nothing

and I mean nothing
impedes flow.

And Yet

It was 17 years ago
that I heard my father utter
his last words.
And yet
I still hear him faintly
in the walls of my soul.

I was an acrobat
in getting free from him.
It took adrenaline and grit.
And yet
I left some things
on the table:

the legs of my teacher,
the shape and their strength;
the arms of my friend that summer;
the curves of women
on Lexington Avenue;
feeling like a boy
shooting baskets in gym.
Fantasies, dreams, longings:
all remaining, all ignored.

I had to prove my father
wrong,
so I spent my life on that.
And yet
in my sorrow,
I must grieve what was never born.

In making sure
he did not own me,
I got distracted.
Revenge is a tricky business.
And yet
I remember myself as a young girl:
she is still in there,
shooting hoops like a boy,
no dresses in sight.

Inheritance

My fourth toe is like my mother's.
I took simple parts of her:
a mouth, some knees,
a birthmark (my sister took my father's),
but above all,
below all,
my fourth toe is like my mother's.

At night
on frozen lonely Minnesota nights
when the hour muddies lines and shapes,
my toe, so like my mother's,
makes me want her to be here.
A picture of her, dressed in summer things,
propped against an icy wall,
looks at me
as if to say:
    It's cold there, I know.
    Spring always comes (it always has)
    and I'm knitting you pretty yarns
    to keep you warm.
    You are my girl, my first girl,
    so far away from here.

I am your girl
no one could say I'm not
with toes like ours.
They are evidence of
my birth from you,
when I took a mouth, some knees,
a birthmark and a toe,
and a way of laughing, of sitting
too complex to explain.

Exodus

Not to be dramatic,
but life is exhausting.
There has been no Moses around
to part the sea;
no staff held up,
no peeling back the tides
to expose easy terrain,
no smooth sailing.
Life, with its comings
and goings,
its entrances
and exits,
its freedoms
and oppressions,
is ours to figure out.
If it's time to leave home,
move out
or move on,
we thrust ourselves
forward
slamming doors
or tiptoeing,
whichever way will
set us free.
We leave in boats,
floating toward new shores.
Or we seek safe harbor
in arks;
two by two
we survive the floods.
Some make a break
bolting from black holes.

Others swim against the stream
or take flight,
heading for the hills
in search of safety,
warmth, a promised land.
There has been no Moses around
to part the sea.
And yet, we have persisted
in our exodus
from darkness to light,
from cruelty to kindness.
Clusters of souls,
we huddle, we hurl ourselves
from here to there
propelled by love
to keep on living.

Relief

Sometimes
out of nowhere
it seems,
I feel the sadness
of a time span
longer than my own.
I begin to miss
people I've never known
and some I know
and never see.

When it comes
(the sadness),
it travels up my spine
and into my eyes
and the tears come
and I say:
Here we go again.

It lasts
only for minutes,
passes
like a warm,
long-awaited spring wind.

Homeland Security

In case you thought otherwise,
I love staying put.
Home is my paradise.
No need for an itinerary or luggage.
The garden is lush and lovely
and the bed,
so inviting.

Cancellation

He called
to say
he would
not be coming in
tomorrow:
"Getting help
is more
than I can
stand
on such a
rainy
winter
day."

Sabbatical

Time stretching out before me
like some highway in Nevada,
a ribbon of road toward a slivered horizon,
no stop signs or billboards.

Another day and then another,
stacked up like a new deck of cards,
ready to shuffle,
ready to play.

Weeks going on forever,
a luxury, indescribable:
wandering, roaming,
no map or obligation.

Minutes flowing into hours into days,
falling off the calendar like petals of a flower,
an endless schoolyard recess,
playing after dark.

I have forgotten I will die someday.
That's the kind of time it is.

Solstice, a prose poem

I'm unsure if the winter solstice is the best day or the worst one, if we're honoring longer days or shorter nights, if it's cold we want less of or light we want more of — which does not surprise me because I was taught by my mother that when you're sad you should feel cheerful, because happiness is right around the corner, and when you're happy, you should feel dread because sadness is lurking in the wings. So forgive me, I am confused.

Is this shortest day of the year to be dreaded or welcomed? I can never decide. I do know this to be true: I like darkness, cold and snow. I don't have the blues when the sun is being stingy; we deserve a major break after summer, the season of enthusiasm, when, if you listen closely, everything is chanting *grow, grow, grow*. I prefer the quiet of winter, the peace that comes at night, the world in slower motion. It is the time of the cave: being at home, inside, under the covers, warm and still.

And yet I like the idea that more sunlight will return, although I think it gets ahead of itself by August, when I say out loud to the sun: *all right, already … you made your point*. As the corn gets high and the tomatoes ripen, I long for the autumnal light that precedes winter.

Happy people bore me, to be honest, just as summer is too much of a good thing. It is the unanswered questions inside the deepest places that make my heart sing. So I am grateful for the dark and for my friends who honor it and gather together on this numinous night of the winter solstice.

No worries for those who prefer more brightness: as of tomorrow, we will slide again toward light, as the earth, slanted on its axis, keeps orbiting the steady sun. The flowers will bloom, the birds will migrate north, the bears will come out from their dens, as will the skunks and, of course, the groundhogs. The queen bumblebees will reemerge, as will turtles, bats and ladybugs. The world will be bustling, movement and mating everywhere.

On a humid sunny day, when the temperature is hugging 100, I will long for this December night: no barbecue, no loud music coming from the neighbor's radio, lawnmowers fast asleep, just lights sparkling like rock candy from trees and doorways, a vast highway of time, perfect for reflecting, for making sure it is still you inside your body. And if it is, then go out and look at the stars in the steely sky, the moon as vivid as it ever gets, shining light, like a trusted friend, on the darkest night of the year.

Snow Day

Like insulation,
the white snow
from the heavens
quiets the din
of grief
even for a day or two.
The snow emergency
is a pronouncement
from above:
snow is everywhere.
Beware of gladness.

Faraway Sounds

turmoil turned low,
treble gives way to bass,

this day, covered in clumps
of quiet snow,

a far-off snowblower
joining acoustical heaven

like a train in the distance,
a message, far away:

life is moving
even when you're not,

like the sounds of
children playing outside

a house where someone
might very well be dying.

Indian Summer Day

This might be the last day
of the warm side of autumn.

The hostas froze the other day
and they lie in the garden defeated.

I switched the thin cotton coverlet for the one made of
down:
a sure sign of what's to come.

One night, a frigid wind blew through the city.
A majestic branch of the red-leafed maple broke and fell
onto wilted wisteria.

But today, the impending change of seasons
is taking a break, the calm before the storm perhaps.

The sun is hot on my face,
which I have positioned, like high-tech radar, toward it.

Eyes closed, body relaxed,
I am storing the heat, or is it hope,

for the next season of darkness,
the frozen world, where the sun appears,

stingy as a seductress,
lighting the sky yet keeping all the warmth for herself.

April

You should have been there:
the day the snow melted
revealing the shamrock green of grass,
a cardinal singing for his love,
the sun high enough to cast shadows.

Before Dawn

Morning, black as night,
sun not yet risen,

as miraculous as a butterfly, emerging
or an infant being birthed into its own breath,

light stays hidden, invisible,
waiting for the earth to rotate,

the sun slowly peeking over the horizon
releasing the splendor we call a new day.

Cat on a Summer Day

My cat spent the afternoon
lying, looking dead,
on the hot concrete of the driveway.
He must love the warmth
radiating into his beautiful body.
I say his name in a tone
I use only for the cats.
It must sound like I am speaking
to small children.
My soft voice,
full of affection,
melts into the driveway.
He barely looks up,
intoxicated, I think,
on this sultry summer day.

Feeding the Birds

It might be the thistle they are after
or the black-oil sunflower seeds.

Their food does not interest me
as much as how they eat,

how they congregate or feed alone,
how they swoop in toward the metal perch,

never missing it or stubbing their claw,
graceful and ravenous all at once.

The civilized cardinals
eat in pairs, first the male, then his wife.

Do they fly back to the branch in the tree
or the wire on the fence

and discuss the meal? Was it superb?
Perhaps better than the feeder down the street?

A clique of sparrows swoops in like sorority sisters,
extroverted and shallow,

eating and spitting out the hulls
as they gossip about the goldfinches.

Oh, the goldfinches! Always dressed for the occasion
in their electric yellow tuxedos.

Dining upside down, the acrobatic olive female
gives the sparrows short shrift.

And so they come: the chickadees, the nuthatches,
the grosbeaks and brown thrashers,

flying in to fill their gullets,
gracing my own little way stations.

They are meant to fly, to follow the sun
and, like pilgrims, they take what is offered.

The Widow's Nap

In our bed
sleeping off the grief
of the late afternoon,
I let my leg splay
toward your side:
I long for the warmth
of our feet playing
under the covers
as we talked
about what to have
for dinner.

To live without
the small
ordinary
gestures of love
is the killer.
It is why I nap:
so exhausted
living this life
lying in bed
without you.

64

We paced out
the number of strides
between the road
and where you are
resting
(as they say),
so that when
the snow falls
we can find you.
Could you feel us
placing roses and juniper boughs
around your grave
on your first birthday
as a dead person?

You said
you'd see your 64th,
living out the Beatles song,
but I still love you
anyway.

You are remembered
every day.
It does not need
to be your birthday,
but since it was,
we got together
and spoke of
all things
you.

Sick Cat

Driving our cat
to the emergency vet,
I say out loud:
where are you?
The cat needs you,
I need you.
Do you have responsibilities
in heaven or under the ground
or in the air
or wherever you are?
Do you take care of children
as you did here?
Do you have pets or
good friends
or does death relieve us
of such earthly cares?
Do you miss anything
or are you
bathing in bliss?

I will somehow get medicine
into our sick cat tonight,
but I need you here to hold him down.
And then once he is asleep
we could get into our bed together
and talk and kiss until we both
fall into a dream.

Grief

My heart aches.
On nights
like this one,
when the moon is nearly full,
and the spring breeze
ruffles over my body,
I can feel it
beating wistfully
as I grieve in and out,
in and out,
remarkably akin to
breathing.

Scar

A memory
as crisp as black ink
on white paper:
his scar.

As I get dressed
before a morning of work,
the image of his torso
flashes on a screen.

His once-smooth body,
opened, interrupted,
flesh healed over the incision
like a zipper.

What was done inside
with instruments, tools,
baptized for an elegant surgery,
saved his only life.

He naps in a pool of sunshine,
scar revealed,
still weary, tender
from exposure.

The Day the Snow
Took Over the Sky

How can a snowfall
make you forget
you are missing
the person you loved
to spend winters with?
It is the heavy
wet, white snow
upon dark branches,
the majestic trees,
shining like royalty,
that cause the forgetting.

Membership

This lake inside the cemetery
is the country club I have joined.
I am a living member
with privileges to sit among the dead
and write poetry till I'm weary.
On a bench near the water,
with an eagle overhead
gliding on thermals
until he dives for the fish,
I spend the afternoon.
Someday I will be buried here.
A lifetime membership,
near this bench,
this lake,
my body will be ashes,
and my spirit will return
as a poem.

The End of the World

If later this week
the end of the world comes to pass,
I'm glad I spent today
arranging deep red dahlias
and a carnival of zinnias.
I have enough tomatoes,
bacon, fresh romaine for
my favorite summer sandwich,
along with ripe plums,
crisp, sweet watermelon
and a big bowl of blueberries
to get me through.

If we are blown to smithereens
on, say, Thursday,
I will have written this poem,
along with my story
about the life and death of
someone I loved,
who, by the way,
will not be suffering
this week's cataclysmic doomsday
since he has taken shelter
in the afterlife or some region
where radiation is irrelevant.

If these are truly the last days
of my life,
I hope each one is
simple and ordinary:
cotton sheets on the bed,
coffee in the morning,

birds at the feeders.
I'm in the middle of a good book,
one of the greatest pleasures,
and the morning glories are blooming
so the bluest blue is everywhere
as I begin each final day.

Well-Being

Maybe it's the light,
oblique, stretched
like golden gauze
over afternoons,
warm sun and
chilly breeze.

Or maybe it's sleep:
right ratio of
hours and fresh air
through open windows,
sounds of trees swaying
shaking loose their leaves.

Or maybe it's just luck,
like finding money
in a pocket,
flash of relief,
brief respite from
striving.

It's feeling
the calm joy of
wanting what I have:
a poem,
a working body, beauty
and, of course, love.

Prose

The Cheating Incident

I was not popular in high school. I was not unpopular either. I operated in a kind of valley between the very smart girls and the very popular girls. Now it is important to note that my school was made up of only girls, and not many of them at that. There were only 18 girls in my graduating class. The school, between Lexington and Third on 70th Street in Manhattan, was one of several New York all-girls schools. It housed about 300 people, girls from kindergarten up to 12th grade, and all the teachers who worked hard to educate them so that they would get into good colleges. I entered this school in the seventh grade. I had spent fifth and sixth grades in a large public school in Manhattan and kindergarten through fourth grade in a suburban public school an hour from the city.

In the seventh grade, I suddenly was taking Latin and French. The classes were tiny. Sometimes there were only eight girls in a class. The teachers expected a great deal from every student. I was petrified. In looking back, the way I coped with my terror was to be funny in class. I was liked primarily, I think, because I had a sense of humor. The funny defense. And it worked. I learned a great deal at that school. But it was not without a huge cost. Not just the money my parents were spending to send me there, but also it took a toll on my developing sense of morality, and on my shaky sense of myself in what was a difficult childhood.

My parents were both professional and worked until late most every evening. My sister and I were kept company and were cared for by a series of "maids" who lived with us. One of these maids is the subject of a story I will tell, but that's for another time. This story is chiefly about something that happened during my senior year of high school, something that I have dreamt about at least once every two or three years since it happened in 1965. My parents play a critical role in this story, though they were not present when or where it happened. My mother was at work, being the New York editor for a large publishing company. My father was a cardiologist, making house calls he resented having to make.

Every night of my adolescence, my mother chain-smoked as she read manuscripts in bed after work. The maid cooked and served dinner, which my parents, my sister and I ate together most weeknights. The dinners were hell. My father scrutinized everything I ate — teased, shamed and intimidated me and was mostly furious. I understand now that he resented most women (his mother, his mother-in-law, his sister, my mother's sisters and even my mother). He also resented the responsibility he had as a physician. All that anger and disdain got displaced onto me. So by my senior year, I refused to come to the dinner table. I ate at 11:00 after they were in bed. My father was livid, and in a dramatic *Who's Afraid of Virginia Woolf*-like tantrum, he told me I would have to start seeing a psychoanalyst because I was causing him "health problems." Thank God I knew to remove myself from his presence at the dinner table. And thank God for the psychoanalyst.

****

At the end of my junior year in high school, the school went through the process of electing the next student council president. In the assembly room of the school, where all the dramatic and musical performances and all the ceremonies happened, there were three enormous wooden ornate placards hanging on a wall. Engraved into the wood were the names of all the student council presidents from the time of the first student council in the 1940s to the present. The engraved names were painted in gold leaf. Every time we assembled in that room, we all stared at those big wall hangings. These were the names of the leaders, the stars, paragons of something or other. Now it seems ridiculous, but then it was hauntingly powerful. So when the school was electing a student council president from my class, tensions were high. The upper school was charged with nominating three people. After that intense process, those three candidates had to lead campaigns in the entire school (including the kindergarten) until the all-school election day.

How or why I was nominated, I do not understand. As I said, I was neither popular nor unpopular. I had few friends. There were some teachers I loved, but they had no role or power in the election. I was sort of that "everyman" candidate, a bit bland, bewildered, awkward. Being in the limelight was totally unexpected. The other two candidates made sense. They were the student council president types from birth. One was exceptionally smart and beautiful; her parents were so wealthy that their apartment smelled rich. Really. The other one was the most popular girl in the school. She also was beautiful, went out with boys (which most of us didn't) and had a reputation for being "fast." I, on the other hand, tended toward nerdy. I was overweight, did well enough in school, but was not a star. I was athletic, but did not excel there either. What I was was funny. And that counted for something. Evidently I was nominated, I suppose, because I was not the least bit intimidating. I was not a threat to anyone. I am sure no one was envious of me. Nothing much to envy. So I was safe — funny and safe.

I campaigned on a platform unlike my opponents'. They were espousing the need for more school dances, increased privileges for juniors and seniors, and a new field trip policy. I was promising, if elected, to abolish the uniform requirement and to institute an academic honor system. Every girl in the school wore a uniform. The lower and middle school students wore plaid skirts and yellow round-collared blouses and the upper school students wore pewter gray jumpers with white, button-down collared shirts. If we forgot the belt or if we wore the wrong shirt, we were supposed to get a detention slip. It seemed idiotic to me, at least the detention part. Mostly though, I was more interested in creating an honor system. The level of competition in the school was steroid-strength and cheating was rampant. I thought that the student council could develop an honor system, wherein students would be responsible for keeping themselves honest. I'm not sure that this interested anyone really, except the teachers.

The election happened at the end of the school year, after all the campaigning was over. The handmade Vote-For-Me signs came down, and makeshift voting booths were put up in the assembly room right under the student council president gilded wall hangings. Defying the odds like a lame racehorse, I was unbelievably elected to be president of the student council for the 1965-66 school year. Everyone was stunned, especially me. I think the following explains how this happened:

> *Vote splitting is an electoral effect in which the distribution of votes among multiple similar candidates reduces the chance of winning for any of the similar candidates, and increases the chance of winning for a dissimilar candidate.*
>
> ~ Wikipedia

So the two likely candidates canceled each other out and there I was, shocked in a sea of shocked constituents. My parents were more surprised than proud. I was terrified. I would return to school in September to see my name carved and painted in gold on the placard in the assembly room.

During the summer of that year, I had a part-time job at The Asia Society downtown. When I got home from work, I wrote poetry nonstop, using my mother's Remington typewriter. I also saw my psychoanalyst (Dr. Mortimer Fromberg Shapiro) four times a week, lying on his couch talking about my life of 17 years.

I prepared for my upcoming reign as president of the school by meeting weekly with the faculty member who was charged with "advising" the president of the student council. I suppose I should use uppercase P, S and C when I write "president of the student council," but that summer I was so scared that lowercase seems even too big.

The advisor's name was Mrs. Holt. She was also the school's college advisor. She was tall and friendly. I could tell she knew that I, as her charge, was one green leader. We talked each meeting about my plans to institute a different uniform requirement and she helped me research academic honor systems in other New York schools. I loved my meetings with her. I knew she liked me, even when I was not using my sense of humor. I think somehow she knew I had a father who was way too hard on me and a mother who was largely not present. I remember telling her about Dr. Shapiro, so I guess I must have told her something about why I was going. I remember feeling safe talking to her. She was an anchor in an otherwise weakly tethered late adolescence.

I did my research about honor systems. So I was prepared, when the school year started, to present to the student council the ways we might institute a system in which every student would take an oath to report any incident of cheating to an honor council. I learned about the necessity and burden of decision making by consensus, the use of the sometimes-awkward Robert's Rules of Order, and the seemingly impossible effort to get an institution to change. But we prevailed, and an honor system was voted on and put into operation before the end of the first semester. All the terms were defined: cheating, complicity, plagiarism, academic integrity. Everyone knew the rules and signed an oath both to not violate them and to report any known incident of academic dishonesty to the newly established honor council. The honor council would be made up of elected class representatives and Mrs. Holt as the faculty advisor.

So here is where the trouble started. I was in a very small

chemistry class with about nine other seniors. The lab was on the top floor of the school. It had a wall of windows flanking five lab tables and counters fitted with Bunsen burners and sinks. The tables were littered in an organized way with beakers, pipettes, graduated cylinders, test tube clamps, mortars and pestles, and test tube brushes. This is where we sat, not just during class, but also during tests and exams. Almost all 10 girls in the class were applying to Ivy League schools. Leah (one of the girls I ran against for student council president) was wanting to go to Barnard. Amy was applying to Wellesley, Iris to MIT, Claire to Princeton. My parents wanted me to go to my mother's alma mater, Smith College, but I did not want to go there. So we were in conflict about yet another thing.

It was a cold December morning when the 10 of us showed up in the chemistry lab to take our final exam for the semester. It was extra tension-filled because we were told that our first-semester grades weighed heavily in the college admissions process. So we took our places at the chemistry tables and the teacher passed out the exams. I was at a table on the far right of the room. I opened the exam and started reading the questions. We were allowed to use calculators, so as I reached to get mine, I noticed four classmates at the counter farthest away from where I was sitting. They were whispering to each other. The teacher was a man who taught part time. He worked in some radiation lab when he wasn't at school and had, attached to his belt, a radiation detector. He was very hard of hearing. He sat at the front of the classroom doing some chemistry calculations at his desk. The four girls started passing notes to each other as they took the exam. My heart stood still. I was watching my classmates cheat before my eyes. I knew I had to report them to the honor council. Or did I? If I reported them, their futures might be changed. Their parents would be furious, the principal would be outraged, I would be hated and accused of treason. But if I did not report them, I would be a hypocrite, a sham, a terrible leader. How I finished the chemistry exam I do not know. I was in tears, under the weight of the first moral crisis of my life.

I went straight to Mrs. Holt's office. The anxiety in my chest was interfering with my ability to tell her what happened. I knew that if I followed the rules of the honor system, I was faced with turning in four of my classmates, that is, almost a quarter of my class. And these girls were among the brightest, their parents were among the largest donors to the school, and I had the rest of senior year to endure the social consequences of my actions. And if I did not turn them in, I would be violating the entire project I had dedicated months to installing. I imagined I would feel like a fake and a fraud and would not be able to live with myself, as I continued to lead the school until my graduation. I knew that these four girls saw me watching them and so they were undoubtedly waiting to see what I would do. I think they must have thought I would do nothing. Why else would they have continued cheating? So if I did nothing, I would likely be immediately welcomed into their group, the popular group, the smart group. If I reported them, I would lose friends and any meager popularity I had. If I did not report them, I would feel more liked by my class, but I would lose something inside of me, inside the awkward chrysalis that was becoming my own self.

I believe Mrs. Holt also saw and perhaps felt the dilemma I was in. I stayed in her office for the better part of the afternoon, long after school let out. The early winter light was steely and joyless. I made the decision to follow the honor system rules and made a formal report in writing to the honor council. There had been only one other report to the council by the end of December, that of a seventh-grader who had plagiarized part of a paper. I walked the 15 blocks to my home. I did not mention anything to my parents. By December of that year, I was no longer joining them in the dining room for dinner, so it was easy to avoid the subject. I told my sister, who was in the eighth grade at the same school. She would be hearing about it most likely before

Christmas vacation started. She said she felt scared for me. I did get the feeling that she thought I had done the right thing. I was unsure my parents would feel that same way.

By the end of that week, my life at school had changed dramatically. The report went to the honor council. They voted and it was decided that the four students involved would get an F in the class. The principal, Mrs. Taylor, was informed about the incident by Mrs. Holt, who was following the honor system bylaws. Once Mrs. Taylor knew, the members of the faculty were informed as well as the parents of the four girls. I need to repeat that these girls were known as some of the smartest in the class. Their parents were major school benefactors. They were powerful in our little universe and they were, for all intents and purposes, exposed and humiliated. And they were furious. The whole school felt inflamed and shaky. I was at the center of the quake and I felt vulnerable, as if maybe I would be erased or run out of the school, my class, my senior year, my little 17-year-old life.

During the next weeks, my parents got involved. They were angry and disappointed with me. They wanted to know where did I get off being my brother's keeper. How could I have done this to my own classmates? They asked what was wrong with me. Who did I think I was? As you can imagine, this put me over the edge. Thank God for my daily sessions with Dr. Shapiro over Christmas vacation. I would walk down the block (his office was conveniently located at the end of our street), and lie down on his couch and cry. He asked me many, many great questions. He never said if he thought I had done the wrong or the right thing (after all, I guess he had that trained out of him), but I had the feeling that he was proud of me. I'm sure this was partly the meaty positive father transference I had toward him, but even so, his office was a sanctuary. How my family got through Christmas that year, I cannot remember.

When I returned to school in January, the four girls in my class had rallied many other students to their side. In gym, when we played volleyball, they got on one side of the net and as they took turns serving, each one pounded the ball with her fist, yelling *Gail D. Hartman*. We all used to do this first semester, yelling the names of the candidates running for mayor of New York. The Liberals would serve by pounding the ball and yelling the Conservative candidate's name, *William F. Buckley*, and the Conservatives would do the same thing yelling *John V. Lindsay*, the name of the Liberal contender. So I was on the chopping block. My parents were not behind me. Almost all the students in my grade saw me as a traitor. The mother of a classmate Ginny Peterson called me one night. She told me how much she respected me and that she was 100 percent behind what I had done. I wasn't even friends with Ginny Peterson. But I certainly felt grateful to her mother. The only adults that expressed their support were Dr. Shapiro, my French teacher, Mrs. Holt and Ginny Peterson's mother.

I heard from Mrs. Holt that the colleges the four reported girls had applied to were informed of the cheating incident. I lived in dread of what would happen to me in school if they were not able to go to any of the colleges they had aimed their whole lives toward. I had applied "early decision" to a college my parents did not want me to go to. It was a small college in Ohio, the first college in the country to admit women and African Americans. To my parents, Ohio was a state in the deep Midwest. The Midwest was regarded as the most boring, inconsequential place in the country, maybe even the world. I think they thought I would not be accepted, since my math SAT score was quite low. They were counting on me to go to Smith, where I might have gotten in due to my mother's legacy. I told Dr. Shapiro that if I ended up at Smith, I would run away. So imagine everyone's shock, including mine, when I heard from my first-choice college in Ohio that I had been accepted, early decision. And I was the first one in my class to get admitted to college. I suddenly felt that the hellish bubble I was living inside had a crack in it. I would be free from this school in six months and free from home in eight months. Getting into college in January was like waking up from a nightmare. I could make it until the following September.

By the end of the spring, everyone in my class had heard from the colleges they had applied to. There seemed to be no consequence for the four girls who were caught cheating in chemistry. They all got into the colleges they wanted to go to. Perhaps Mrs. Taylor, the principal, never reported anything to the colleges, or maybe the colleges didn't care about what happened, or maybe money had had an under-the-table role. I was caught between feeling relieved that my actions had not played a part in their future academic lives, and feeling confused. What good was an honor system? Did it teach anybody anything that mattered? Everyone in the school observed that cheating had a negative consequence, but they also saw that it might be helpful in getting good grades and it might not deter anyone from getting into the college of their dreams. I lost the few friends that I had. I was shunned by my classmates until I graduated. Going to school every day was like hell. Was paying this high a price for doing the "right thing" worth it? I imagine that the inner turmoil I would have felt had I not reported my classmates would have been costly in another way. That would have been, however, between me and myself. This outcome affected every strata of the school. The toll on my own adolescent psyche is still hard to measure. And of course, I am unaware if it had any positive outcome for anyone involved. It wreaked havoc in my family; yet, I suppose we got through it or just went on.

On the day of graduation in June, the seniors processed into the assembly room with *Pomp and Circumstance* playing over the loudspeakers. We took our places on the stage. The faculty sat to our left in rows perpendicular to us and the parents and family members sat in rows facing the stage. The cameras were flashing. The wooden placards on the walls were lit by little lights mounted on the tops of the frames. There, in gold, were the names of the leaders of the school since the school was established. The last name on the list was mine. I couldn't believe that the year was finally over. I sat on the stage imagining graffiti on the placards: *Run for the hills* or *This school is a joke* or *Who wants to be the next sucker on this placard?* or *Free at last.*

Before we got our diplomas, there was an awards program. Each department head rose, went to the podium on the stage and announced the best student in his or her subject area. Believe it or not, two of the four reported girls got awards: one for English, and one for history. The crowd went wild. The parents of the girls stood up and cheered. I knew I would not be receiving an academic award. As I said, I did not excel in school. I did fine, but nothing special. I was not awards material. At the end of the academic awards, a shocking thing happened. Mrs. Holt got up on the stage and said that she was giving out an award on behalf of the entire faculty, to a senior who demonstrated courageous integrity and most contributed to the culture of the school. And then she said my name. I was stunned. My face was hot. The entire faculty stood up and applauded, and then slowly, the audience reacted. I looked out at my parents. When they saw the faculty giving me a standing ovation, they, too, stood up. And a few other parents were on their feet, as well. I walked toward Mrs. Holt and took the award — a plaque — from her outstretched arm. And then she embraced me, right there in front of everyone. I felt as though I had been air-lifted to a different world for those minutes on stage.

After graduation day, I never once walked inside that building or saw one student from my class again. I have been able, in recent years, to Google the four girls I reported. I was only able to find three of them. One is a well-known modern artist who has work at the Whitney Museum and the Museum of Modern Art and several museums in Europe. She married a composer who wrote the music for many notable Broadway musicals. Another is a patent attorney in Manhattan and lives on Park Avenue. And the third teaches history at Columbia University. I was not invited to join the school's alumni association. I suspect no one in our class was asked to join. The cheating incident was a dim chapter in the school's history.

I wish I could say there is a moral to this story, a lesson to be learned. There is neither, I'm afraid. In the 50 years that have passed, I have thought about the cheating incident hundreds of times. I decided long ago that I did the right thing in reporting my classmates, adhering to the honor system and to my oath to comply with it. But I still wonder if doing the right thing was worth it. Was anything gained? My last year at home was more miserable than it would have been, I lost the few friends I had, I was bullied and humiliated. I witnessed something very dark in my parents' reaction to me that took years to get beyond. I lived with a kind of loneliness that I can barely let myself remember. What I think the ordeal gave me — and to some extent, still gives me — is a firm belief in ambiguity. Nothing is ever perfectly good or perfectly clear, not even honor, honesty or integrity. Life is complicated and murky. Occasionally, maybe for moments at a time, there is true clarity. But mostly, I find life to be a series of tangled, complex, many-layered events. There is no true north. Justice happens as much as corruption does. Dishonest people get elected to positions of power. Goodness prevails, but so does evil. And then someday we all die, having tried to make sense of all the polarities, having tried to tolerate the ambiguity of all life as long as we could.

The Standing Appointment

The beauty parlor was one-half block from my school. Every Thursday, my mother arranged a "standing appointment" for me to have my hair done. I was 12. The shop was not a fancy one, not the one my mother went to weekly; it was a small neighborhood beauty shop whose name I can't remember. The smell inside was sickening: the perfumed chemical odor of perm solution and the electrical smell of hot hair dryers. The man who did my hair was short and he wore his thinning hair slicked back. His hair was wet and shiny and he smelled like lime juice. He always looked at me as though I were on a temporary leave from a locked ward somewhere. Before he set my hair, he washed it in a green molded plastic sink. The hot water felt good on my scalp and as long as I kept my eyes closed, it was pleasant. After the shampoo, I would sit up, open my eyes and feel dread about what was to follow. He would stare at my scalp, putz around in his drawer of rollers, and roll clumps of hair around each bristled tube. Then I would get up, go to a row of dryers and sit for what seemed like half my life. Under the hot plastic dome, I watched the beauticians shampooing, cutting, perming, bleaching, drying, setting, combing and brushing hair. The customers were all women, mostly older than my mother. They were coming there willingly. They liked it. They liked talking about their friends and relatives while the beauticians fussed about their heads. Will I want to do this when I grow up? I doubted it. Eventually, the man came to turn off my dryer. I walked with him to a chair way in the back of the salon. Rarely was anyone else back there. As I stared at myself in the mirror, he removed the rollers and brushed my hair. I hated the way I looked. I hated the canned curls, the fake waves, the stilted shape. But that was nothing compared to what always came next. Each Thursday, at the end of my appointment, the man took a book of matches from his pocket. He lit one match after another, holding each one up to the ends of my hair. He was singeing my hair so that it would grow thicker and prettier. He was singeing my hair so that I would be a better daughter. He was singeing my hair to erase me, to punish me, to incinerate me in the hopes that a new, different girl might emerge. The odor of burning hair must be what hell smells like: a dry smell of dead body parts, a smell of disappointment, a smell of the whole universe burning. When he finished with the last match, he always said: *All done. Much better.* I never saw another person get their hair singed. If I ever knew whose idea this was, the singeing of my hair, I have long since forgotten. I do remember, though, that every Thursday evening at home, my mother would say that my hair was looking much thicker and I was looking better and better.

Alice Kramer

Alice Kramer and I were two of four Jewish girls at Pine Cone Camp in Pocono Pines, Pennsylvania. We came from New York City where the other two Jewish girls lived. One of them was my sister and the other, Alice's cousin. The remaining 150-plus girls were from Pennsylvania — mostly around Philadelphia, Wilkes-Barre and Scranton. It was a green secluded camp for girls run by a Quaker couple, "Miss Peg" and her husband, "Mr. Cox." It was during my summers at camp that I learned some of the most important things I know: that I am likable, that looking at the moon at night could give me a sense of safety and hope, and that things that live — like trees, dogs, grass, horses and flowers — are what you can count on more than anything else.

I met Alice at camp when I was 11. She was four years older than I, and if she is still living, she is now 75. She had very strong arms and legs and a gait that looked uncomfortable, her knees bumping against one another with every step. When she wasn't talking, her face fell into an expression that made me think she had seen all the sadness that the universe had ever offered.

Alice played the guitar so magically that everyone at camp stopped what they were doing and came to listen when she picked up the instrument. This was right before Joan Baez and Bob Dylan became well known, the renewed popularity of folk music not quite into its own. Alice's fingers strummed the strings of her guitar with such sensitive intention; her music was like a sound that the rhythm of the earth was calling forth. And no one could resist it. She and her guitar reminded me of the Pied Piper and his flute. Alice gave me my first folk music album — Peter, Paul and Mary — and their music later carried me, or I carried it, into my adulthood. Their sound was Alice times three, and the records I have of theirs are the most tangible connection I have to Alice Kramer.

She was more than my friend. She was like a cousin/sister/alter ego, a person I could make a difference to by just being with her. We were not best friends; we were certainly not inseparable. We were like cards in the same deck: the queen of hearts and the queen of diamonds. She understood what I was only on the verge of being able to grasp about myself: that I would be a survivor of my troubled family, that I would be able to bring forth some depth within myself at critical moments (which would save my life), that I would be able to create lifeboats with which to reach the shore.

Alice herself lived in a kind of mysterious darkness. What I know about her is this: she called her parents by their first names — and always had. They were like her sister and brother, and she was their only child. She lived on the Lower East Side of Manhattan and had friends and followers of all ages and persuasions. She participated in the part of New York that was only a story to me. I knew the city's forehead, the city's cheekbones; Alice knew New York's crotch, its loins and thighs. When she was depressed, she retreated, like a sullen sleepy animal, into a cave. When I looked into her eyes, I saw her despair; actually I saw all women's despair, my own, my mother's, my sister's. Her eyes were haunting and beautiful. In the dark, almost black irises, I could see that she doubted her survival, that she was uncertain she would ever find a place where she could feel at home.

Twice when I knew her (each time during the winter in New York), she tried to kill herself. Both times she slit her wrists. They (her sister/mother and brother/father) took her to Payne Whitney, New York's most well-known psychiatric hospital. She called me many times while she was there. They kept moving her between two floors — from the third to the fifth to the third to the fifth. On the fifth, she could neither make nor receive phone calls. She told me later that the fifth floor was a locked ward. She liked to show me her scars. They were smooth and bumpy, the way the cuts healed. They looked like small sections of a city road map. Every time I saw the scars, I felt how close I was to impending loss, to thwarted hopes, to giving up, to going into my own despair, my private place where I would allow no one to enter — so that no one could ever leave.

During my last summer at camp, when I was 15 and Alice was 19, we were camp counselors together. Our cabin's name was Hideaway and we lived with seven six-year-olds, seven little girls from Pennsylvania. It was a magical summer and I loved the children. One was terminally homesick, and Alice and I took turns staying up and holding her until she cried herself to sleep. Another one talked in her sleep, and Alice and I would awaken and listen to the mosaic of the child's mind. Alice played the guitar and sang the kids (and me) to sleep each night. It was really quite wonderful.

One night during that summer, it was raining very hard and the wind blowing through the cabin was cold. We got up in the middle of the night to cover the children with extra blankets. I returned to my bed, and as I began to fall back to sleep, I felt someone next to me. It was Alice. She got under the covers and lay down with me. The front of her body — her belly, breasts and face — pressed up against my back and head. She put her arms around my shoulders and sides and we just lay there. I reached for her hands and held them. We stayed like this, half awake and almost completely still, for the rest of the night. I don't remember when or how she got back to her own bed. We never once talked about that night. And it never happened again. But I do remember how her body felt next to mine. It felt safe and warm, like hunger satisfied. It was secret and sacred, and somehow I knew I shouldn't tell anyone it happened. And I never have.

In 1969, when I was away at college, my mother called to tell me that Alice Kramer was being interviewed on *The David Susskind Show*. They were talking about the riots in Greenwich Village and the gay liberation movement. My mother said she looked the same as she did at Pine Cone Camp and then asked, "Did you know she was a lesbian?" And I said I just knew she was Alice Kramer and I was glad to know she wasn't dead.

Sometimes I wonder why on earth I dated men. God knows my most profound and loving relationships have been with women. I was always attracted to women; I loved reading books with lesbian characters, and I never really liked many men. They often seemed so foreign. But when I met the man whom I later married, we talked the way women talk. We connected, but we were separate in some way that brought me safety. When I looked into his eyes, I didn't see my own suffering, my own despair. I saw that life is not always a complicated struggle, but rather something you can count on: waking up in the morning, with the odds greatly in your favor that you could have a very fine day.

Grace

When I was entering the first grade, my parents moved from Manhattan to Westchester County, specifically to Irvington-on-the-Hudson, about an hour north of the city. I imagine they moved because they wanted to have the best of both worlds: easy access to the city they loved and a peaceful place to live in the country. My mother resigned from her job as an editor at a major publishing company, and my father, a cardiologist, was going to commute to his practice and hospital, both in Midtown Manhattan. We lived in a white stucco house at the end of a cul-de-sac. My mother got a part-time job doing freelance editing for a writer named Carl Carmer. He lived a few towns farther north on the Hudson and was known for writing about the rivers of America. I believe she edited his book called *The Susquehanna*. My father left the house very early every morning. He often stayed in the city if he had been called in the middle of the night to make a house call. Medical care was very different in 1954.

My sister was going on three when we moved to "the country," as they called it. And I was starting grade school. So my parents hired a live-in caretaker and housekeeper. She also did the cooking. I barely remember her, partly because she turned out to be one of several people my parents hired. It seemed that there was always something wrong with each of them, something they did too much or not enough of. One was fired because she stole my mother's cigarettes. My mother chain-smoked Chesterfields and she bought them by the carton every few days. She became a three-pack-a-day smoker. And yes, she did get lung cancer, but that was not to happen for 30 years. She went to Carl Carmer's large home and office many days a week, so the housekeeper they hired was with us more than either of my parents was. As I said, there was a series of them. One of them was a great cook, but had a drinking problem. Another left without notice. We woke up one morning and she was gone. Her room was cleaned out; not a trace of her remained. She did not even stay for her paycheck. I believe my parents did their due diligence and looked into their references and job histories. These women came with baggage and more needs than we ever had.

Now let me say that hiring a live-in housekeeper (who was called a "maid") was a common practice in New York. I assume it still is. My mother was raised by an Austrian governess in the '20s. Her name was Miss Baumann and she took my mother and my two aunts to St. Patrick's Cathedral every day for Mass when they were children. It is important to note that my mother's family was Jewish. I have no idea if her parents knew or cared that their three daughters were practicing Catholicism on a daily basis. Until the day my mother died, she went into Catholic churches to light candles whenever someone was sick. And during my early childhood, she sent our outgrown clothes to Miss Baumann's family in Austria. My father grew up in a poor section of Queens on Long Island. I believe he felt his hiring a maid for our household was a feather in some money cap he wore. He married into a class he did not come from and this fueled much of his determination and, quite frankly, his aggression, throughout his adult life.

After living in Irvington for five years, we moved back to the city. The commute was very hard on my father, and my mother was itching to get back to full-time work as a book editor at her publishing company. It was a hard transition for my sister and me. We loved playing in the woods behind our Irvington house and we had lots of friends on our street. But we did not get a vote, and back to Manhattan we went. My parents bought an apartment on 85th Street between Madison and Park Avenues. We moved during the summer after I finished the fourth grade. The building we moved into had two doormen, and the apartment had living quarters behind the kitchen for whomever my parents were to hire as the next maid.

My mother crafted a small ad to be printed in the classified section of the *New York Times*. I believe this is how, in 1958, families found the maids and nannies who lived with them. She stated that we were a family of two professional parents and two small children, living on the Upper East Side. She must have included that the apartment had separate maid's quarters with its own bathroom. So one day, as we were getting settled back in Manhattan, I remember my mother being unusually excited about a letter she received from a new prospect, a woman named Grace Waldman. The letter was handwritten and her precise penmanship was exquisite, almost like calligraphy. It was written in pencil on beautiful cream stationary. The postmark was from Greenwich, Connecticut, an hour or so from the city. Grace Waldman said that she was very interested in being considered for a live-in maid position in our household. She described her last work setting: a family in Greenwich with two children in a large home. She wanted to leave the family because she said she could no longer witness the degree to which the parents were spoiling their children. She described them as unbearably entitled and she could no longer stay in their employ. So Grace was looking to relocate to Manhattan.

The editor in my mother was over the moon about Grace's letter and how she described her life and her work experience. She was born in 1923 and her mother died in childbirth. She and her older brother, Tom, were raised by their father, who was a chauffeur and butler for a wealthy family in Connecticut. They lived and grew up in the carriage house behind the estate of the family her father worked for. My mother immediately invited Grace to come to the apartment for an interview and to give her a chance to meet us. There were no references to check because Grace did not want the family she was leaving to know she was looking for another position. She was plain-looking and yet, rather beautiful. Her hair was brown and cut in a true Buster Brown/pageboy style, with shiny, perfectly straight bangs. She wore brown pants, a beige sweater and had a creamy camel's hair coat hanging over her arm. We were charmed by her. She seemed to love the apartment and she was very kind to my sister and me. My parents hired her on the spot and she lived with us for the next four years.

Grace was unlike any of the maids we ever had. And she would prove to be unlike anyone who followed her. First of all, she was Caucasian. Most maids at the time were either African American or Hispanic. She told us all about her early years, living in Connecticut with her father and brother. Grace was 35 at the time she started living with us and she had very little family. Her father died when she was in her late 20s. Her brother and his wife lived in Decatur, Illinois, and they had two children: her niece, Stefanie, and her nephew, Sam. Other than the four of them, she was alone in the world. She had a depth of knowledge about art, ballet and history that belied her lack of education. She finished high school, but her father could not afford to send her to college. In the mornings, before my mother left for work, she and Grace often talked about the theater, ancient art or literature. They were both fans of Willa Cather, Edith Wharton and the poet Anne Sexton. My mother was in awe of her intellect.

I was fascinated by everything about her. She looked like a character from a book, petite and precise, like her handwriting. Her chestnut brown hair was cut perfectly and there was never a hair out of place. She wore a taupe and ivory long-sleeved uniform most of the time with a cream-colored apron that matched her fabric belt. The shape of her body looked almost as if she had been molded. Her figure was well-defined in this shirtwaist dress. She was proportioned so exactly, no midriff peeking over her belt, her tummy perfectly flat. Her legs were slim and smooth, covered most of the time by flesh-colored nylons. Her shoes were brown, like her sweater and her coat. Actually, most everything she wore was a shade of brown, her favorite color.

Grace did the cleaning and the cooking. She made my parents' bed every day after they left for work. My sister and I made our own. She did the laundry and the grocery shopping, as well the cooking for the four of us and for my parents' dinner parties. When they had people over, she wore a slightly fancier dress uniform, a darker taupe one with a stylish long-sleeved blouse. She was stunning at the same time as she was almost invisible. She made some dishes that my father loved and asked for repeatedly. One was a zucchini casserole that had crispy breadcrumbs as a top crust. She also made delicious rice pudding and baked small buttery cookies to go with it. She was skilled in the kitchen, and often told us about all the dishes she made for the family she worked for in Connecticut.

She came to us when we lived on 85th Street. She got us ready for school every morning and walked us to PS 6, three blocks away. My sister was in kindergarten and I was in the fifth grade. I hated the school and had few friends. Grace rescued me, in a way, since she often had great activities planned for us when school was over. My parents got home late and we never ate before 7:00. Sometimes my father was absent, having been called away to the hospital for an emergency. I often wonder if Grace was aware of the tension that filled our household. She never talked about it to me directly, but she must have heard my parents arguing. My father had a very volatile temper. And when he was disappointed with anyone (my mother, President Eisenhower, a patient or me), he tended to raise his voice and express his unabashed rage. Disappointment led to anger in him, not sadness. So the tone in the household was governed, in large part, by my father's moods.

The older I got, the more aware I was of an algorithm at play in our family: the more successful my parents were and the more money they made, the more discord there was in the house. Both of them were in highly competitive jobs where they had to handle the high expectations of cardiac patients, in my father's case, or well-known, temperamental writers, in my mother's. When they got home at night, those high expectations transferred seamlessly onto my sister and me. One evening, after I balked at their request that I turn out my lights and go to sleep, my father bellowed: *You should be ashamed of yourself. You're acting like a child.* I was 11.

This was the family Grace Waldman joined and took care of from 1958 to 1962. Two years into her time with us, my parents decided to move from our apartment on 85th Street to the top three floors of a brownstone on 82nd Street. They were elated at the possibility of this move. When they went to look at it for the second time, they took Grace with them. She came home and drew to scale the layout of our next home on blue and white graph paper. The six-story building was owned by Lillian Hellman. She lived on the second and third floors and we were to live on the fourth, fifth and sixth floors. Three bedrooms were on the fourth floor with two bathrooms and a dressing room for my parents. On the fifth floor, there was a living room, a small kitchen, a dining room and a tiny patio that opened onto a study. And on the sixth floor, which was similar to an attic, were the bedroom and bathroom for Grace, plus several storage closets.

We moved during the summer of 1960. I would be changing schools in the fall, entering seventh grade at a small private girls' school. Grace loved the house on 82nd Street. I often went up to her room at night after she finished the dishes and after my parents went downstairs to their bedroom. She would show me pictures of ancient art in her large art history books. She taught me about mythology and about the Lascaux caves in France. One evening she taped some large pieces of poster board to the walls and set up some paints with brushes so we could copy the Lascaux cave horses, stags and bulls. We outlined them first in pencil and then we painted them in shades of her favorite color, brown. The Lascaux cave project went on for a week or two. I loved my time up on the sixth floor with her. She told me stories from her childhood, growing up without a mother and relying solely on her father and brother. One night when my parents were out to dinner, and after my sister was asleep, Grace and I made cocoa and sat in the living room and talked about death. She said she wanted to live to the age of 39, no longer than that. I was 12 at the time and 39 sounded pretty old to me. I was too fascinated by her to be very concerned. She seemed to know so much about so many things. And she made art come alive.

Our home was two blocks from the Metropolitan Museum of Art. Grace took us there after school many times a week. When we went to the Egyptian art wing, we looked at ancient hair combs and amulets, scarabs and stone implements. At home, she would have us look at our plastic combs and see how they were descendants of the Egyptian pieces. We looked at terra cotta figurines and amphorae of ancient Greece. On the way out of the museum, we would stop at the shop and buy a postcard of something we had seen that day and take it home and make drawings of it before we put it in a folder labeled Greek Art. She went through a period where all we looked at were the paintings of Mary Cassatt: all those mothers and children. I often wondered if Grace wished she had children. I thought she was the best mother I had ever had, even though I knew she was not my real mother.

Grace's niece and nephew, Stefanie and Sam, lived in Decatur, Illinois. They were the daughter and son of her brother, Tom. She spent a week or two with them every summer at a small resort in Rhode Island called The Tiny Barn. She told us many, many stories about them. They were one and two years older than I was. She sometimes sent them a package and wrapped each gift perfectly, with elegant wrapping paper. Endlessly creative, it seemed, she made her own cards and folded envelopes out of paper she saved from beautiful art magazines and catalogs. Once she made a birthday card for my sister's eighth birthday. The card was bound in brown thread and it had four pages. On the first page, one hand-drawn person says to another hand-drawn person: *Alison's 8!* The number eight is cut out of a piece of shiny blue paper and glued onto the card. On the next page, the person who receives this news says, *Oh, no, Alison's ate!* On the third page, the original person says through a hand-drawn megaphone: *No, Alison's 8, not ate!* And then on the fourth page, both hand-drawn people scream: *Alison's 8! Happy Birthday!* Grace always made cards for Stefanie and Sam for their birthdays, Valentine's Day and Christmas. I thought she was the most devoted aunt in the world.

In the eighth grade, we read *The Pilgrim's Progress* in English class. This is a Christian allegory written in the 1600s by John Bunyan. It tells the story of a man named Christian who is on a journey from his hometown (called the City of Destruction) to heaven (called the Celestial City). He is confronted with dozens of challenges and difficulties — which makes sense, since this is an allegory about life, death and redemption. It is very dark and heavy, full of symbolism and characters who anthropomorphize Sloth, Presumption, Mistrust, Diffidence, Hypocrisy and Charity. Christian eventually finds a wife and together they travel over land and sea, through the Valley of Humiliation, the Hills of Difficulty and Danger, the City of Vanity, and the Slough of Despond. You get the picture, I'm sure. So we had a final project at the end of the year, wherein we had to create an artistic or written representation of our understanding of the allegory and present it to the class. Grace came up with an idea to lighten the heaviness of the book. She helped me create an edible *Pilgrim's Progress*. We cut a wooden board to form a base on which we would put nine freshly baked sheet cakes. This created a 27" x 39" blank "canvas." We then frosted our canvas of cake with dark chocolate icing, because after all, this was a dark book. We decorated the massive brown cake with all kinds of edible things to show Christian's journey and all his obstacles. The Hill of Difficulty was made of icing (built up high like a hill) with shards of broken hard candy resembling sharp glass. The Slough of Despond was a swampy-looking pool of muck, helped by food coloring and pieces of raisins and cut-up prunes. The Delectable Mountains that Christian climbed were clumps of gumdrops, the tops of lollipops and angular pieces of rock candy. And the River of Death was fashioned out of strings of black licorice. I could go on, but suffice it to say that Grace and I had a fabulous time. I got an A and my classmates enjoyed eating the intense book we were made to read.

My parents not only worked long hours, but they also took long vacations away from New York and without my sister or me. They went to Jamaica in the winter and to Europe in the fall. So we got to stay with Grace, which actually was what we preferred. In hindsight, my parents' trust in her was enormous. They would leave the country for two weeks at a time, their children in the hands of their hired maid. There were no relatives around for backup. What if one of us had gotten sick? I guess they knew Grace could take care of anything that would come up. She was really our third parent. And as sad as it might sound, I might have liked her the best out of the three.

During one of my parents' vacations, Grace took us to see her favorite ballet, *Giselle*, performed by the American Ballet Company. It is the story of a beautiful peasant girl who falls in love with a count who has disguised himself as a fellow villager. Giselle learns of his deception and realizes that they will never be able to live their lives together. She proceeds to fall apart and descends into madness. It is a story, basically, about unrequited love. Grace owned a boxed set of records of *Giselle* and she gave me the liner notes to read about it before we went. When I got to the ballet itself, I was spellbound. I had only been to *The Nutcracker* and so this felt like a new experience, a grown-up ballet. We went to a matinee performance on a Sunday afternoon and when we got home, Grace played the LPs on the stereo. I read from the libretto while my sister and Grace, having changed into leotards, danced in the living room.

The only thing we knew about her own love life was that she occasionally went out on her days off with a man named Don, whom she called her "beau." He picked her up outside our building in a taxi. I tried, sometimes in vain, to peer out the window to catch a fleeting look at them driving off. Once, from five stories up, I saw them embrace before she got into the cab. Don was a handsome man from what I could tell, dressed in a suit and tie each time I caught a glimpse of him. Grace did not talk about him at all — I had no idea what he did or where he was from. We somehow knew not to ask. Grace and Don seemed mysteriously matched, almost like their love affair existed in some other galaxy. Don was like gossamer — he was real, yet somehow insubstantial. And Grace, alongside him, looked diaphanous and fragile. I was glad she had a suitor, and a life outside of our household. I never thought she would go away, even though, looking back on it, why wouldn't she? Don seemed like a steady, reliable presence in her life even if she did not see him often. It must have been my wish to have her stay in my life forever that prevented me from thinking she might someday leave us.

In the summer of 1962, before I returned home from camp in Pennsylvania, my sister accompanied Grace to The Tiny Barn resort in Rhode Island where Grace and her niece and nephew were spending a week. My sister had a wonderful time and when she returned to New York, she told my parents and me that she liked Stefanie and Sam. She especially delighted in telling us that they had a nickname for Grace — which was "Mom." So she started calling Grace "Mom," as well. When my father heard that, he shot my mother an uneasy look. Now my father, even on a good day, was a suspicious man; I might even say a bit paranoid. He was also eerily intuitive so his paranoia was often veiled by his tendency to be accurate.

This was the beginning of the end, though we did not know it at the time. My father, one Sunday afternoon soon after he heard about Grace's so-called nickname, lay on his bed with the tome of the Manhattan phone book beside him. Grace had an efficiency apartment on the Lower East Side where she went on Sundays, her day off. He opened the phone book to the page where he found dozens of G. Waldmans or even a few Grace Waldmans, and he started dialing the numbers. He listened to the voices as each person answered the phone. No one sounded like Grace. Then he played with the spelling of Waldman: G. Waldmann, G. Walldemann, and finally G. Wahldmann. Like a dogged detective, he called every one of the names, and after much of the afternoon — bingo. Grace answered the phone. She was listed as G. Wahldmann, W-A-H-L-D-M-A-N-N. Of course my father said nothing into the receiver. He simply heard her voice and hung up the phone. He looked satisfied, as though, after an afternoon of hunting, he had brought home the kill.

My father was not subtle in his growing suspiciousness. One night at dinner, while Grace walked around the dining room table serving us from a large platter of broiled fish, he asked her about where Stefanie and Sam went to school. Out of the blue. The following evening, again while she was walking around the dining table serving us from a bowl of broccoli, my father continued his investigative line of questions: *What company does your brother, Tom, work for? How long has he lived in Decatur, Illinois? Any reason you haven't gone to Decatur to visit them?* I felt dizzy. Grace had to be seeing through this. What was my father trying to prove? Who cared if she lived a secret life? Why was he exposing her, embarrassing her?

Over the next two weeks, something changed in our household. I was less welcome in Grace's room after dinner. She became rather distant and withdrawn. My mother was angry with my father for incriminating Grace, for pummeling her with unanticipated questions, for carrying on a not-so-covert investigation. I wondered if he got what he wanted when Grace came back to our house after her next day off, with a shocking haircut. It was extremely short, in a pixie style, with pointed side burns and blond streaks. She was not wearing brown, but rather a plum-colored skirt and a navy blue coat. It was like seeing Santa Claus sporting a Mohawk, wearing a blue jean jacket and corduroys. It was horrifying, in the way that clowns are horrifying.

I was distraught. What was happening to my surrogate mother? She was slipping away, no longer reliable or interested. She looked as though she were another person, not the Grace we loved and needed. I had trouble sleeping. Something was very wrong in the house. I hated my father for upsetting the balance. I hated him for pushing Grace away — which is what happened. Within a few days of the haircut, she announced to all of us that she was going to be leaving us to marry her "beau," Don. My mother found it within herself to be congratulatory — after all, this was a wedding announcement. My father followed suit with a self-satisfied string of well wishes. I was stunned. I felt as if someone had punched me in the chest. It was hard to catch my breath. I could almost feel my heart breaking. If Grace left, how was I to make sense of anything? How would I make it through the next four years before I could be free and leave for college?

She gave my parents two weeks' notice. During that time, she talked with a great deal of animation about marrying Don. She said that they might move to Decatur, so she could be closer to her brother and her niece and nephew, Stefanie and Sam. I was in so much grief at knowing she was going to leave, that I became remote and less interested in knowing about her plans. Even though my mother said she was leaving to create a better life for herself, I felt that Grace was abandoning us. If she loved us, would she be leaving us for a man she rarely saw? Was her love for us real? Was Don real? This plan to marry him came out of left field.

On the day she departed, my mother asked for an address so we could send her flowers on the day of her wedding. She gave us only a PO address, which of course was proof to my father that she was a fraud. He later said that flowers could never be delivered to a post office, and since she left no phone number, there would be no way to reach her. She gave us a hug goodbye, got on the elevator and was gone. I went into my room and closed the door and cried myself to sleep. It felt almost unbearable.

We somehow went on with the week. My mother was going to take some time before trying to find another maid. We were old enough, she said, that we did not need to find someone right away. So I came home from school to a barren house. Once I went up to Grace's old room. It was emptier than empty. In the closet were her tan and taupe uniforms, ironed perfectly and hung on wooden hangers. I smelled them and stroked them, feeling the smoothness of the cotton. They looked just like her except without her body. Maybe she left them, I thought, because she might come back. It was almost impossible to believe she had gone away.

One evening a week later, after dinner (which my mother cooked) the phone rang. I was doing my homework and my sister had gone to sleep. I heard my mother make a loud noise, a combination of a scream and a groan. I ran into their bedroom and my father told me to go back to my own room and he shut their door behind me. I lingered in the hall and heard my mother crying and my father talking to someone on the phone. I could not make out the words that were being spoken, but I knew something very bad had happened. He hung up and I tiptoed back to my room so as not to get caught eavesdropping. My mother kept crying; the tones of their voices were urgent and intense. I had to know what had happened, so I boldly walked down the hall and knocked on their bedroom door. They said I could come in and they closed the door behind me. They said they would tell me what happened, but made me promise not to tell my sister. They said she was too young to understand.

The call was from Tom, Grace's brother in Decatur, Illinois, the father of Stefanie and Sam. Shockingly, we found out that night that Tom was actually not her brother at all, but was really her ex-husband, and Stefanie and Sam were their children. He called to tell us that after Grace left us, she went to The Tiny Barn resort in Rhode Island and committed suicide, shooting herself with a handgun. The police called Tom and he came from Illinois to identify and bury her body. He called us a few days later. Grace was 39, the age she told me she would not live beyond.

Standing at the foot of my parents' bed, I was hearing that Grace was dead, that she killed herself and that she was the mother of Stefanie and Sam. For that moment, the world did not make sense. It was also very disturbing to see my mother cry. Her sadness was so often shrouded by her cerebral and vaguely cynical experience of everything. My father looked stern and angry, which was not at all unusual. I was in shock. I began to sob when it registered that she would never be coming back to get those uniforms upstairs. My mother hugged me and I can still almost smell her nightgown wet with tears and smelling of cigarettes. She kept saying she was so sorry. I wondered what she was apologizing for? Was she sorry that I lost someone I loved? Or was she sorry that she had relinquished her maternal care and responsibilities to Grace?

A few days later, my father informed me that, according to Tom, Grace had been in a "sanatorium" for alcoholism many years before she came to us, and that she had been diagnosed with schizophrenia. I did not believe that then nor do I believe it now. Grace had one drink every night while she cooked dinner. She did not drink in her room. She was never inebriated. Even my parents agreed with that. Perhaps in 1962, "schizophrenia" was the catchall term for any severe mental illness. People with schizophrenia are markedly disorganized in their thinking, speaking and behavior. They are often agitated and unfocused. Characteristically, they neglect personal hygiene and lose interest in everyday activities. Their movements can be jittery and their speech is often jumbled or overly rapid. Most people with schizophrenia struggle with the basics of daily life. None of these symptoms describe Grace. She was highly organized, focused, engaged with us and with the world in very appropriate ways. She was neat as a pin, articulate and clever.

The grief I felt, the utter emptiness of life without Grace, the horror of imagining her shooting herself, the tan and taupe uniforms hanging in her closet, the sudden pixie haircut — everything seemed bleak and muddled and I retreated into my room, closing my door as soon as I came home after school. It took several months before my mother put an ad in the paper to find the next maid. Since my mother worked until 6:00 or 7:00, she did not start preparing dinner until almost 8:00. I had been home for four hours before either of my parents arrived in the evening. Many times I refused to join my family at the table. I was sullen and angry, which displeased them. They wanted me to buck up and to stop moping. My father said that I needed "to get on the ball" and put the past behind me.

I missed Grace so deeply and I had no one to talk to about what had happened. I had promised not to tell my sister. I was too scared to tell a friend or even a teacher. It all seemed so horrible and confusing that I could not imagine how I could ever share the story of Grace with anyone. My parents did not want to discuss anything about her. I was alone in my head with my memories and with my curiosity. Who was Grace? What was her real life story and why did she invent an alternate one? I have carried these questions with me over my lifetime. After all, she was almost my mother for four years. And it was Grace who lit a fire under me about art, creativity and, in her death, about illusion.

I began doing research on Grace Wahldmann's real-life story after I left college. I must have needed to escape the burdens of my family and the household that was once enlivened by Grace's presence and then shut down by her death. I ruminated for years about the stories she told us. Finally, and over many years, I pieced together the true story of Grace's life, a story she stored privately, under the surface of the life she led with us.

The family she said she worked for in Connecticut before coming to live with us was most likely imaginary. Because she said that she did not want them to discover she was pursuing another job, my mother never asked for references. All those culinary dishes she said she cooked for that family were, most likely, either made up or ones she cooked for her own family. Grace told us she and her older brother were raised in a carriage house by her widowed father who was a butler and driver for a wealthy Connecticut family. In truth, she was raised in her own well-to-do family by her mother and father, with three other siblings. She was the second born, her older sibling being a sister named Vivian. She had two younger brothers, neither of whom was named Tom or Thomas. Her father was a prominent attorney in New Haven, Connecticut. Her mother did not die in childbirth, but rather outlived her by 12 years. Grace was not uneducated, and in fact, attended Wellesley College.

It was while she was in college that she met a man named Thomas Wahldmann. He was from Decatur, Illinois, and they married in 1943. They stayed in Connecticut after the wedding and eventually moved to Decatur after their daughter, Stefanie, was born in 1945. In my search for who Grace really was, I found a picture of her and baby Stefanie in the *Decatur Herald*. It was such a shocking photograph that I gasped when I saw it. Grace, looking young and beautiful, appears frozen and dour. She is holding on her lap a tiny baby swaddled in a lacy blanket. Little Stefanie looks as grim as Grace does. In fact, Grace looks like she is barely touching Stefanie, who is basically propped on her lap. The joylessness in this baby announcement photo was jarring.

A year later, Grace and Tom Wahldmann had their second child, Samuel. There was no photo accompanying baby Sam's birth announcement in the paper. The year was 1947. Five years later, when Stefanie and Sam were five and four, Grace made a suicide attempt in a hotel room in Chicago. She slashed her wrists, but was saved by the police before she died. The newspaper article said that she and her husband, Thomas Wahldmann, were divorced at the time of the attempt. So the marriage must have ended when the children were toddlers. I have never been able to unearth where Grace lived or where she was hospitalized in the years before she came to live with us in 1958. I assume she lost custody of her children.

Yet many things have fallen into place. When Grace was with us, we never saw her arms. She always wore a long-sleeved shirt or a cardigan sweater. We did not know it, but she was hiding the scars on her wrists. Her favorite ballet was about a woman's descent into madness. And all those birthday, Valentine's and Christmas gifts, so perfectly wrapped for her niece and nephew, were for her own children. I now understand why we repeatedly visited the paintings of Mary Cassatt at the Metropolitan Museum. Mary Cassatt, an Impressionist painter in the 1800s, painted intimate portraits of women, particularly of mothers and children. It was no accident that I went on to major art history in college, by the way. I believe to this day that my interest and curiosity about art stems from Grace's taking me to the Metropolitan Museum so many times after school. When I was studying art in college, I came upon this description of Mary Cassatt's work by an art historian: *Her constant objective was to achieve force, not sweetness; truth, not sentimentality or romance.* I think Grace was trying to figure out the truth about her relationship with her own children, whom she called, rather tragically, her niece and nephew.

The two men she told us about (her brother, Tom, and her boyfriend/fiancé, Don) were invented. They were both really her husband, Tom. I imagine he came to New York on business every once in a while, and they got together — perhaps to talk about Stefanie and Sam. She must have had his permission to take them each summer to The Tiny Barn in Rhode Island. I have often wondered what tale she spun to Stefanie and Sam explaining who my sister was that summer they spent a week together. Did her children know their mother was a maid? Grace's own family in New Haven employed a Polish maid to live with them for much of her childhood. And the prosperous Wahldmann family of Decatur might well have employed a housekeeper. How would her children have understood that she was living as a maid, taking care of another family's children? She probably invented some inverse fiction for them. Did they understand why their mother did not have custody of them? And finally, if her husband, Tom, thought she was an alcoholic with schizophrenia, why would he have allowed the children to spend time alone with her in Rhode Island during the summers?

My curiosity about the real Grace is tempered always by my memory of who she was with me. I know I deeply loved her during the tender years of my early adolescence. And I know that so many of my choices in life, from what I studied in college to the career I chose to pursue in psychology, relate to my relationship with her. In many ways, she gave me a way out of my intense, unhappy family. She showed me what curiosity looks like. She taught me, for example, not only about the history of the Lascaux caves in France, but also about the doing of art, the painting that any of us can do at any time, even on paper taped to the wall. I felt welcomed into her interests, which were so alive, kinetic and infectious. Yet this Grace, this version of Grace, could not live in her own family, so instead she lived in mine for four years. She was, in the end, not who she portrayed herself to be. She was a figment of her own imagination.

And so I loved an illusion, a fascinating chimera, a person whose mind created an alternate universe, one she could endure for a few years. In the desert, if the air is hot enough on the ground and cold enough aloft, you see a mirage, a beautiful body of water, an illusion produced by the reflected light against the sky. And if you are very thirsty, you go toward the mirage as though it's real. You imagine drinking the cold, radiant water that is just ahead of you. You can almost taste it. You begin to love it. It gives you hope. It feeds your imagination. It gets you through. Grace was my mirage. When I went toward her, I could see her looking at me, looking into me. I could see what she was going to teach me. I could feel myself loving her. I started to experience the relief from loneliness, the awakening of creativity inside me. And when she disappeared, as mirages do, amazingly I had what I needed to survive without her.

Leaving Lillian Hellman

When I was entering the seventh grade, my family moved three blocks, from 85th Street to 82nd Street in Manhattan. This sounds like a small change, but it was enormous. It was a sea change, like moving from a pond to an ocean. On 85th, we lived in a three-bedroom apartment in a 28-story older building with elevator men and two elevators. I was told not to talk to anyone in the building, except the elevator men (which sounds crazy: the elevator men could have been recently released from prison for all anyone knew) and to never cross to the other side of Madison Avenue. I always wondered what could happen crossing to the other side. Was it the street that was dangerous or were there child molesters lurking on the other side?

So during the steamy summer preceding seventh grade, we moved to the top three floors of a six-story brownstone on 82nd Street owned by Lillian Hellman. My parents were buoyed by this move in a way I did not understand. My mother kept talking about how exciting it would be to live above Lillian Hellman. All I knew was that Lillian Hellman was notorious for hating children, evidenced in her play *The Children's Hour*. I worried for myself and for my younger sister. The elevator in the house was no bigger than a small broom closet. It was paneled with mahogany and mirrors and it smelled like sweet citrus. The elevator took us to our floors, the doors opening right into our apartment with no hallway or even vestibule from the elevator to the front door. So the sound of the elevator, which was always audible, signaled the comings and goings of any one of us or of Lillian Hellman. It was a game my sister and I fabricated: keeping track of the comings and goings of our landlord and her strange children-hating guests. We made up stories about where she had been, about her relationship with Dashiell Hammett (who was to die a year after we moved in), and who her friends were.

My mother and father loved living on 82nd Street. I did not. It was across the street from my old elementary school, which I despised. Everything about living there left me lonely. My parents went to work early and returned home late. Lillian Hellman was only heard from at night. And the caretakers of the building, who lived on the main floor, kept to themselves. They burned incense all the time and they had a sweet round baby. I believed they were vegetarians, which intrigued me. I knew for sure Lillian Hellman ate lots of beef. Her face looked like an artifact the first American astronauts had brought back from outer space, all craggy and cratered. Her eyes were like slits bookending her colossal nose. Her head was much too large for her small body, but I figured she needed such a skull to house her massive, brilliant brain.

In the afternoon after school, I wanted to either hide in my room or escape the building altogether. I often walked two blocks (by the age of 14, I was allowed to cross the Avenues, specifically Madison and Fifth) to the Metropolitan Museum of Art. There, I would go downstairs, past the Egyptian tombs and mummy artifacts, under the medieval tapestries, and finally past the petrified ram head from 3300 B.C., which was found in Mesopotamia (to be honest, I often paused before this piece because it had an eerie likeness to the head of Lillian Hellman), and on down the surgically immaculate marble stairs to the Children's Museum. There I would wander among the dioramas of farm scenes from the Fertile Crescent, the harvesting of maize and the handmade tools of ancient worlds. I discovered in this museum within a museum lovely places to sit, benches covered in olive green velvet, museum turf. I would get comfortable and watch small children with their parents or nannies, on the verge of tantrums whining for food or freedom.

In a well-lit and secluded alcove on the other side of the dioramas was a life-size replica of a Greek statue of Zeus. He stood there every day, on a black stone slab, with his arms outstretched from his broad muscular shoulders and his legs straight and wide apart, almost as though he were going to do a jumping jack. His head was turned to the right, as if gazing toward something very important — like the truth. I began to visit Zeus with some regularity. He was predictable and interesting. I went to a girls' school and so did not know any boys and had never seen a boy without clothes, except my cousin David when he was an infant. His little penis was like a dollhouse fire hose, the way his pee would arc all over his legs when my aunt changed his diaper. So imagine my shock when I was eye to groin with Zeus. When I stood before him, my eyes were exactly at the level of his private parts, which were, quite frankly, not so private. Hundreds of people looked at him every day. His body made me worry — about my body. It would never work: it would never fit. Why hadn't my mother told me? I would never be able to have children; no one would want to marry me. I would be alone and adrift my whole life. My visits with Zeus became serious and intentional. I began to march over to the museum in the afternoon after school to absorb the entire horrible situation. I would stare at him, at his enormous, gargantuan groin and try to imagine what I would do with the rest of my life.

We ate dinner late, around 7:30 or 8:00. I would slink home around then, crossing the previously dangerous Avenues, down 82nd Street to the building where I lived. I would open the heavy ornate door and enter the front hall and walk to the minuscule elevator. I would press the button. The little moving room that smelled of freshly peeled lemons or oranges would take me up, past Lillian Hellman's two floors to our home. I would get off the elevator on the fourth floor, across from the kitchen and join my family for dinner. I was not a quiet child, they tell me, but I know I never asked them about the size of Zeus and the size of me. And curiously, they never asked me where I had been. I wondered if I was in a bad Lillian Hellman play.

So imagine the joy, the outright ecstasy of leaving this strange house and the neighborhood where Zeus and Lillian Hellman resided when I left for college. Amazingly, I met real boys there. My roommate was from Montana and only knew about Zeus from her mythology class in high school. Lillian Hellman was studied in English classes, but I never let on that I slept above her my whole adolescence, trying hard not to absorb the peculiar pessimism on 82nd Street. Here, in college, I was far away from all that hollow loneliness, eye to eye with people just my size. I loved the feeling I had when I looked out my window at the unfamiliar view of green lawns and people milling about in excited conversation with one another. I thought about Zeus now and then, and it occurred to me more than once that I had been focusing on the wrong part of his body. I should have paid attention to his turned head, his pointed finger. He was gazing and pointing toward the right — or the west, toward the country beyond New York. He was trying to tell me to leave the museum, 82nd Street, Lillian Hellman, my family and New York altogether. He was saying: *Run. Run for the hills while you can.* And I'm glad to this day that I did.

My Mother, A Cautionary Tale

My mother, like yours, was not always my mother. Long before I was born, the stage was set for the experiences I would have being raised by her. She, as well, had a mother and father who had not always been her parents. The same was true for her grandparents, and on and on. Who were these people, our parents, before we existed, before they even had the slightest notion they would go on to have children? I have been curious about this question since the day my mother told me sex is unsanitary.

I will begin at the end of her life at the age of 88: she was so phobic about death that the hospice nurse at her bedside called me up in the middle of the night, 1,500 miles away, to ask if my mother was a victim of the Holocaust. She said that they only see the kind of extreme resistance to dying that my mother was exhibiting in people who have been horrifically traumatized. My mother, Joyce Frankel Hartman, lived in Manhattan when Adolf Hitler became the prime minister of Germany. When Germany invaded Poland, she was 17, starting college in Northampton, Massachusetts. And she lived in New York City, married to my father when World War II ended. They lived in a small apartment overlooking Gramercy Park, which was nowhere near Germany, Poland or Austria. So no, she was not a victim of the Holocaust.

My mother was the oldest of three daughters of Sylvia and Joseph Frankel. She was born in 1921. She told us Joseph was a brilliant and successful stockbroker, holding a seat on the New York Stock Exchange. Sylvia was a woman of leisure in her early years. Despite having endless time on her hands, she hired an Austrian governess named Miss Baumann to live with them and raise the three children. My grandparents were Jewish; Miss

Baumann was a devout Catholic. She took my mother and her sisters to St. Patrick's Cathedral on Fifth Avenue every day of the week. They attended Mass, took Communion, and lit candles for the relatives of Miss Baumann in Austria. As an adult, married to my father (also Jewish, but nonobservant), my mother went into Catholic churches and lit candles for anyone she was worried about. Needless to say, I grew up confused about organized religion.

As my sister and I outgrew our clothes, my mother would pack them up to send to Miss Baumann, who returned to her native country after her employ with the Frankels. I believe the clothes were worn by Miss Baumann's nieces. My mother never lost touch with her. She was closer to her governess than to anyone in her young life, though she downplayed the connection when she spoke of it. My grandmother Sylvia was a cold and peevish woman, perhaps lonely in her marriage. She died when I was 12, so I did not know her for long. Mainly I remember feeling afraid of her. My father disliked her intensely and they often had angry interchanges on the telephone. Sylvia was always looking for a reason to criticize him, since she believed my mother married "beneath" her. And he gave Sylvia plenty of fodder, although surprisingly not in the area of social standing. He was a cardiologist, so he got many points for his ability to provide and for his stature as a physician. But he was resentful, petulant and provocative. My scary grandmother had met her match. I realized at an early age that my mother had married her own mother.

Always wanting to be a writer, my mother took a job after college at *Look* magazine, where she authored a few articles and edited many others. This is where she worked while my father was stationed in the Philippines as a Navy doctor. When the war ended, he returned to New York to complete his residency in cardiology at Roosevelt Hospital. In 1946, she got a job at Houghton Mifflin Publishing Company, where she worked until her retirement in 1979. She took off a few years when my sister was born, but otherwise, Houghton Mifflin was her other home. She worked her way up the publishing ladder and spent the last 15 years of her career as the New York editor of adult fiction and nonfiction.

My mother read all the time. She brought home manuscripts in typewriter paper ream boxes and sat in bed, reading and marking up the pages of someone's writing. I often wondered if she would rather have been the writer than the editor. She was endlessly critical and opinionated. Occasionally she invited her published authors to our home for dinner. My sister and I were permitted only to greet these guests upon their arrival and to say goodnight to them before we went to bed. I used to eavesdrop on their conversations from a safe distance on the stairway. If an author was from a foreign country, my mother's accent would change, and she sounded as though English were her second language. I have no idea what my father thought of this. Perhaps it was ultrasophisticated behavior, but to me, it was false. One hundred percent affected and artificial. I wondered why she needed to become a pseudo-Frenchwoman, a bogus German, an ersatz Swede.

As my father became more and more successful as a doctor, he was at home less and less. He made house calls after his office and hospital hours. The phone would ring in the middle of many nights, followed by the murmuring of his voice, the click of the receiver being put back on the phone cradle and then his bellowing: *Jesus Christ! Goddammit!* After a few minutes, I would hear the front door of the apartment slam shut. I imagine that all those years he was seriously sleep deprived, which did not help his proclivity for irritability and abusive language. My mother slept through his middle-of-the-night tantrums, which annoyed my father to no end; he needed all of us to know how much he suffered doing his job. She stayed up later than he did every night, chain-smoking in bed, lost in reading manuscripts. She lived in her own private world of literati, Chesterfield cigarettes and syntactical errors.

Nurturing was not a word I would use to describe her. Given her upbringing, I suppose this is understandable. She was driven, sophisticated and competitive. She wanted the best for my sister and me in a conceptual way — and she loved us as well as she could. She tended toward being unreachable and preoccupied, as though immersed in a desperate drive to stay moving forward, never looking back, never reflecting. My warmest memories of being with her were at night, when she would take her bath. She would soak in a hot tub with her cigarette in hand, a washcloth floating on top of her breasts. She allowed me to come into the bathroom and sit on the closed toilet seat. It was from the vantage point of the bathtub that she talked to me most candidly. This is not to say she was open. She was just more communicative than at any other time. Still, even with our bathtub chats, I could find out very little about her life before I was born.

These are some of the things I learned about her at the edge of the tub:
- she loved Smith College
- she disrespected her sisters
- her mother worked as an interior decorator after Joseph died
- she adored Adlai Stevenson
- she loved Graham Greene's novels
- she disliked my father's sister
- she admired Anne Sexton, who she said committed suicide
- Sylvia Plath went to her college
- she wanted me to go to her college
- she was engaged to be married to someone before she met my father (I could not find who broke off the engagement or why)
- she did not breastfeed me

- she had no intention to stop smoking, saying: *If I quit
  smoking, I'll get hit by a truck*
- and, as I said earlier, she informed me that sex is
  unsanitary

The more money my parents made, the fancier the parties they
attended. They dressed to the nines for these soirées; my mother
wore a perfume on those nights that I still associate with being
left alone in the apartment with my sister and the maid who lived
with us. We were allowed to bring dinner to our rooms on those
nights — not that we all ate together most of the time anyway.
Several years ago when I was in a large department store, I went
to the perfume counter and smelled all the French perfumes,
seeing if I could find the one she wore when she got all dressed
up. Sure enough, *Joy* by Jean Patou. It took me back like an
express train to those nights when they went out, looking like
movie stars. They were at the top of their game: a beautiful pair,
successful, smart, a literary-medical couple. In pictures of them
at this time, my mother looks radiant and sophisticated, and my
father, dashing and proud.

In truth, they were coming unraveled. But no one knew it quite
yet. My father was not enjoying medicine, and my mother was
stressed with more and more authors and deadlines. When my
father turned 60, he wanted to retire. It was his chauvinism, no
doubt, that led him to convince my mother to retire first. How
would it look for a man to give up the brass ring before the woman
did? In September of 1979, my mother left the publishing world.
There were a few big retirement galas given in her honor. Then
on a Friday, her last day, she came home, got into bed, and stayed
there for close to a week. She went into a sudden intractable
depression.

Here was a woman, who never for a day seemed clinically
depressed, who stopped functioning on a dime. I was living in
Minnesota by this time, and my father called me frantically; he

was ashamed of her and how this mental health crisis reflected on him. She stopped eating and was started on antidepressants, which had no effect. Then she was hospitalized — in the same hospital where my father worked. He was wild with rage and panic. After a couple of weeks with no improvement, my mother underwent 16 sessions of electroshock therapy. After she was discharged, the only place she wanted to go was to Minneapolis to see her first grandchild, my daughter, Emily. When she arrived, she was regressed, acting like an enthusiastic adolescent. She was impulsive in her speech and actions, swearing like a sailor. Her sophistication was still there in spurts, but she had a sort of what-the-hell attitude, something I had never experienced with her. She did not pay much attention to her baby grandchild other than wanting to buy her little dresses and booties.

After a few days with us, they returned to New York. It took about six months for my mother's familiar temperament to return. When I suggested that maybe a therapist could be helpful in understanding this depression she had fallen into, my father reacted as though I were recommending cyanide. And so, they went on living in the city until my father's retirement a year later. Then they moved out to Long Island, to a little township west of the Hamptons, called Remsenburg. Three years after this move, my mother fell into another depression, seemingly out of the blue. Again she was hospitalized and underwent electroshock therapy, though this time at Stony Brook University Hospital out on the Island. She was intermittently psychotic with this depression, which I call D2.

There were four in all. The following one (D3) was six years after the second one, and the last one (D4) was less than a year before she died. At 87, this final depression was like the grand finale at a fireworks display: fully psychotic. One of the saddest places on earth: a psychiatric hospital unit full of psychotic senior citizens. The only treatment that pulled her back into equilibrium was shock therapy. My father had died before D4, so I got my way and found her a female psychotherapist in a neighboring town. My mother reluctantly agreed to talk to this woman, whose name was Cindy, and claimed throughout the rest of her life that it was not helping. She said they talked about Cindy's children and the colleges they were applying to. I often got calls from my mother telling me about Cindy's terrible taste in furniture, paint color and window treatments. Since I am also a psychotherapist, she compared me to Cindy endlessly. She called and left me messages such as: *Don't tell me you have slipcovered furniture in your office.* And *Are your rates higher or lower than Cindy's?* She said on more than one occasion that psychotherapy is useless and a sham.

I never knew my mother to reveal much about her deepest self to anyone. Toward the end of her life, I harbored a wish that she would use the process of psychotherapy to understand and come to a sense of peace about her history. I was operating on the belief that if we don't understand what our lives have been about, if we don't grieve and accept our disappointments and losses, then we are more likely to die in despair, with a frantic and chaotic resistance to letting go. Cindy was my best hope. Yet my mother used Cindy in the way that she used her friends: as a companion for all things external, as an accomplice in averting attention away from the heart of the matter.

My mother rarely talked about death, and certainly not her own. I would wager that she never thought it would happen to her. She was a master of changing the subject and an expert at dissembling. She must have had compartments in her brain made of titanium with locking devices suited for the Swiss National Bank. Her father died when she was a sophomore in college and no one, neither my father nor my sister nor I, could ever get her to tell us definitively what caused his death at the age of 60. She was forever vague, saying things like: *Oh, he had a bit of pancreatitis.* Or *Why do you need to know? He died in his sleep.* Or *I think he had a heart attack.* When we pressed her, she got irritated and dismissive. His photograph was the largest framed picture on her dresser, five times the size of other family photos. I was born on Joseph's birthday and so they gave me his middle name; I thought this would have given me special dispensation, allowing me access to the truth about how my grandfather died, but it did not.

One afternoon, six years after my mother died, I checked my email and there was an announcement from the *New York Times* Subscription Division: as a subscriber I would now have complete access to their archives. This sounded intriguing to me, so I opened up the link and started looking up my parents' obituaries, my high school basketball team stats and the headline on May 8, 1945, the day World War II ended. Then it occurred to me, *Look to see if there is anything about your grandfather, Joseph Delwyn Frankel.*

I found a gold mine — or in this case a sinkhole — of information. I fell down the rabbit hole of research, joining ancestry and genealogy websites. My mother's father was not the benevolent, extraordinary patriarch described to me throughout my life. He was a white-collar criminal, wanted for a time by the FBI. There were articles about him, not only in the *New York Times*, but also in over 50 other papers around this country, Canada and Europe. My grandfather was not a stockbroker exactly, though he did have a seat on the New York Stock Exchange. He was the owner of a business called J.D. Frankel and Co. They bought and sold diamonds and precious gems. This was news to me.

He was born on May 4, 1888, in New York City. His parents were of German and Polish descent, which flies in the face of what I had been told all my life: that my grandfather's ancestors were from Great Britain or Wales. (I had never heard anywhere about Welsh Jews, though I once looked up the population makeup of Wales and sure enough, there are many small Jewish communities in South Wales.) At the age of 28, in 1916, he was awarded a seat on the New York Stock Exchange. By this time, he had already been married to a woman from Baltimore with whom he had a daughter. His first wife divorced him on grounds of "desertion" and eventually he married Sylvia, though it was not announced in the paper. It was the first I had heard that my mother had a half-sibling.

In 1929, when his children were eight, five and one, he lost his entire fortune, worth $3 million, in the Stock Market Crash. And in 1933, my grandfather was expelled from the New York Stock Exchange on charges of crimes similar to insider trading and embezzlement. This was a scandal at the time, which is why it was written about so widely. He then disappeared, deserting Sylvia and his young daughters. After four years of hiding from the FBI and the Missing Persons Bureau, he surfaced one summer Sunday afternoon at the apartment he had abandoned. My grandmother and her daughters were having a birthday celebration for Sylvia. My grandmother, so relieved he had returned, listened to him explain that he had been hiding in Miami, "pushing an invalid in a wheelchair" for $18 a week. In Sylvia's excitement about his return, she called the FBI to say that they could call off the search, that Joseph had returned to their apartment. She also told them that he had been suicidal during his disappearance. Little did she know that she had inadvertently turned him in to the Feds. The police and FBI went to the apartment straight away, arresting him and taking him to prison.

On June 4, 1940, Joseph Delwyn Frankel died. There is no obituary, no notice of his death. I believe that it was neither pancreatitis nor heart disease that killed him. I believe he killed himself. In 1990, when my mother's youngest sister was sick with lung cancer that had metastasized to her brain, she told me that her father had jumped off the Brooklyn Bridge. I remember asking my mother about this, wanting her to corroborate this piece of news. But my mother said that my aunt's brain cancer was causing her to confabulate ridiculous stories.

The shame around his losing his net worth, his expulsion from the Stock Exchange, his deserting the family, his disappearance for four years, his imprisonment and his suicide must have been so enormous that my mother, Joseph's oldest daughter, ended up deserting herself. She constructed her own reality, excising memories and experiences that were unbearable for her to carry; she created a life with a vibrant, productive career, an identity that distracted everyone, herself most of all, from the reality that her father was not a good man. I will never know for sure, but I think that when my mother learned of her father's suicide while she was in college, she dove as deeply into her studies as she could. She probably wrote short stories with characters from broken families, perhaps with themes of lonely children, sudden poverty and the pressures of war.

There is a saying: history repeats itself. Perhaps this explains why, in 1987, my mother was arrested for shoplifting a carton of cigarettes and a chicken from the local grocery store. My aunt, my mother's youngest sister, called me to report that this arrest was noted in their local Long Island paper. I was completely floored: my mother, a woman who had plenty of resources, who flaunted an air of forced sophistication, trying to steal cigarettes and a chicken! Once I had this information, I was not sure what to do. I decided to ask my father about it several months after it occurred. He was not willing to discuss his thoughts about why she did it. He was simply livid that I knew about it and made me swear to never let my mother know what I knew. I kept my promise.

My mother was a closed system for so long that when her time was up at Houghton Mifflin, when she lost her identity as the New York editor, when she looked into a future with no distractions, when she realized she would spend the rest of her life with her angry, critical husband, she turned inward where there was no functional core. She had edited not only books, but also her life's narrative, her history. She crossed out facts, she rewrote chapters, she changed the storyline. And then when it all quieted down and she was alone with no role to step into, she fell apart.

When I was a little girl, my parents said I was always asking questions, often annoyingly so. At four and a half, the story goes, they took me to the beach at Coney Island. I asked so many questions (such as, *Why can't I drink the water in the ocean? Why is the sky blue? Why can't I touch the clouds? Why is the sand cold when I dig a hole?*) that my mother finally said firmly: *Because that's the situation that prevails.* I think the reason my mother's catchall answer did not deter me from a lifetime of asking questions is that I picked up all the curiosity she disavowed.

Sometimes, on her birthday or when I am making a recipe of hers, I silently thank her for my life as a curious person, having chosen a perfect profession for my temperament. She taught me, by example, that there is a large price to pay for a life lived, yet unexamined. Shame is a killer, but refusal to face it, to understand, is a plague. Our souls cannot be tricked. We cannot do an end run around coming to terms with ourselves. I could have told the hospice worker who called me in the middle of the night, that my mother was not a victim of the Holocaust, but rather a victim of her own disaster. She was refusing to die, I believe, because she knew she had never lived congruently with her real self. Her life, while rich in so many areas, was one of truancy. She tried to run away, to defect. Yet in the end, we all meet our maker, something I'm sure Miss Baumann had tried to teach her at St. Patrick's Cathedral. Death won, of course, and she died with a ballpoint pen in her hand, hoping to edit the ending of one final page.

Westward Ho

When I was 22, I married Danny Weaver in a church in Oberlin, Ohio. This was noteworthy for several reasons. Number one, I am Jewish, and so marrying in a church was a rebellious thing to do. Number two, I married Danny Weaver for his mother. He was a nice enough person, a good friend actually through most of our years in college. But it was his mother I was in love with. She lived southwest of Norman, Oklahoma; she had a Southern accent and was the warmest, most loving woman I had ever met. I wanted to be related to her. And number three, I got married the day before I graduated from college, so that on my diploma my name would read Gail Weaver rather than Gail Hartman. I wanted nothing that was related to my father attached to my future. I had had enough of him in my past.

Now let me say that these are not good reasons to marry someone. But I did, and it lasted just short of three years. Being married to Danny Weaver was not that bad; it just was not that good. He and I were a little like sludge. We did not have the kind of energy needed to propel us into adulthood. But we gave it a try, living the first year of married life in Washington, D.C. It was 1970 and we had spent our four college years protesting the Vietnam War. With the help of a draft attorney, Danny got out of serving in a war he did not believe in, because he had, among many things, flat feet. So he got a job in D.C. as an elementary school teacher. He was the only white teacher on the faculty. I had a job in the book department of the National Geographic Society. The main thing I learned working there was that those stunning photographs were airbrushed (a forerunner of Photoshop, no doubt) and so, while beautiful, they did not necessarily reflect reality. For example, in the original photographs of gypsy women (taken for a book on the subject), there were flies swarming around their heads. Gypsies are not known to bathe frequently and, therefore, are often seen in a cloud of flies. But by the time the photos were published in the book, the women were sanitized, not a fly in sight. In a book we were doing about a male gorilla, the photographer took a picture of him standing upright, with his gargantuan testicles drooping down to his knees. But in the book, this gorilla is pictured as a eunuch. I remember seeing the photo editor's crayoned comments on the proofs: *Kill testicles*. And so, the gorilla was transformed into a neutered primate.

Unfortunately, my life with Danny Weaver could not be air-brushed. After one year, we decided to move to an unlikely place: Grand Forks, North Dakota. In 1971, there was a lot of press about a Graduate School of Education at the University of North Dakota. A Harvard professor had started a program there to train teachers in Open Education. North Dakota had the largest number of untrained teachers in the public school system of any state in the country. So his idea was to train those teachers at the University in Grand Forks while sending trained graduate students out to the empty classrooms for their field placement experience. It worked beautifully and attracted many people from all over the country. Danny applied to the program, was accepted and so we drove our car, complete with our very pregnant cat, Alice, and a U-Haul trailer in tow, across the country to Grand Forks.

Now, this move of ours worried my parents. I grew up in Manhattan, and my mother and father, like most New Yorkers, did not know where North Dakota was located. They knew it was far away, somewhere in the middle of the country. My mother feared, on the one hand, that I would not have access to good health care, and on the other hand, that I would not be able to find Dijon mustard for cooking. Danny's parents were accepting of anything, and saw our journey westward as a fine adventure. I was delighted to leave the East Coast and did not really give my destination much thought. I was moving to leave somewhere, while Danny was moving to arrive at a new place. It also pleased me, in an adolescent way, to be renouncing New York and the entire East Coast. I was done with that part of the country. Grand Forks, North Dakota, in my mind, had to be a better place than New York, New York, or Washington, D.C.

After driving through Maryland, Pennsylvania, Ohio, Indiana, Wisconsin and Minnesota, we arrived in Fargo, North Dakota. We turned right and drove due north to Grand Forks. We had no place to live, figuring we would find a rental as soon as possible. So we needed a motel for a few nights. We used a AAA directory of motels in the upper Midwest to find one that was not expensive and one that would allow a cat. The one we chose was on the edge of town, called The Westward Ho. As we approached it, I thought we were driving onto a movie set for a Western film. The parking lot looked like a livestock corral — split-rail fencing with wagon wheels and lariats as decorative elements. The sign pointing to the front office depicted a cowboy complete with boots and spurs, his rifle pointing to the entrance.

What happened next was distressing and unfamiliar to me. The person at the front desk was standing underneath a skull of some animal and he welcomed us to The Westward Ho. He showed us to our room, overlooking the "corral" and told us how to access the local news and weather on the television, which was high up on a precarious-looking bracket above the bed. He told us about the Happy Hour they offered in the bar, where we could get free "bull fries" with the purchase of a beer. I asked him what exactly bull fries were. He said: *They are the fried testicles of North Dakota bulls — and ours are the best in the state. Sometimes we mix them with pig testicles and those are a treat, too.* When he left us in our room, I was aware of my fear of this new place and of my fatigue from the trek across the country. I went into the bathroom to get cleaned up before collapsing on the bed. I could not believe what I saw on the toilet. There were stirrups from a

Western saddle attached to the seat. I screamed. Danny came in and he told me to look at the phone on the wall above the toilet paper. It was a Western Electric oak hanging crank wall phone, the kind I remembered on *Gunsmoke*. I suddenly felt sure we had made a big mistake with this move.

Danny was very calm and suggested we get a little sleep before evaluating our situation. So we lay down on the bed and turned on the news. There, in the background of some news story, was the Capitol in Washington, our old home, a place that I did not like much, but suddenly longed for. And as I started crying quietly, the weatherman came on the screen. His name was Dewey Bergquist and he was standing in front of a United States map, holding a very large round object that I thought might have been an explosive of some sort. I had never seen anything like it before. He said it was a giant rutabaga from Rolf Bertelson's farm outside of Minot. It was the winner of the local station's Rutabaga Contest. This bulbous root looked like it had hepatitis, it was so waxy and dark yellow. Dewey had a bit of a smile on his face, but I would not say it was an expression of delight or excitement. He then turned to the weather map and said flatly: *Well, no big deals around the nation.* I started crying again and stopped momentarily when I saw the commercial for a John Deere combine. I had never before seen a rutabaga or a combine and I could not imagine eating a bull's testicles. I felt as though we were in a foreign country.

If someone had told me then that I would be in North Dakota for the next six years, I would never have believed it. My time there started at The Westward Ho with Danny Weaver, and six years later, having grown into adulthood, I would leave with another man. I did not know then that I would learn about the sky and the stars and wide-open spaces. I would discover the prairie, something I never once heard spoken of in New York. I would endure winters that were severe and dangerous. My inauspicious beginning at The Westward Ho never hinted at the depth of experiences I would have nor the wonderful people I would get to know. I could have left Grand Forks and returned East to a more familiar city after that combine commercial, but I marvel that I had the foresight, or maybe just the perseverance, to stay. It was in small-town North Dakota, an alien and unfamiliar place, where I discovered more about myself than I ever did in my Big Apple hometown.

The Toaster Oven

It is easier to leave a marriage, even a brief one, when you are angry. Or furious. Or disgusted. I would never recommend leaving a marriage in a state of sweet nostalgia, or even in the ambiguous mood of regretful relief. Yes, if you are going to get divorced, have a really good fight. A righteous skirmish or an outright blowup. A tiny, cranky argument will not do. A few little digs and snipes will fall short, as well. I am talking about a row. I am talking about the kind of dispute that, if you were in a bar, the bartender would say: *Take it outside.*

If my marriage to Danny Weaver had been a balloon, I can honestly say it was never fully inflated. It was companionable and polite. It was serviceable in most areas of life. What it lacked, however, was buoyancy, lightness, passion, agency. Our relationship fizzled into a flabby, toneless union. The marriage ended reasonably with a minimum amount of heartache. I was most upset that I would no longer be related to his wonderful mother. But just as marrying someone for his or her mother is ridiculous, so is staying in a lifeless marriage just to have a great mother-in-law.

So when Danny got into a doctoral program in New Jersey, we decided that I would not go with him. I would stay in North Dakota, in our small rented house. I would keep Alice, the cat. He would take the car. We had little else of value. So on the day of his leaving, an unexpected pall hung over our last morning together. There was a sadness that had its origins in the mistake we had made getting married in the first place. There was pain in knowing that it did not feel worse. When matter is inert, it is motionless. And to leave each other, we needed some action, some energy. So on his way out the back door, he said, *Oh, I forgot the toaster oven.* I said, *Why do you think it's yours to take? I want the toaster oven.* In the kitchen on the yellow Formica counter, there sat, plugged in, the Hamilton Beach toaster oven that his mother had given us when we moved into our little house a year and a half before.

I'm not even sure I ate toast, but I did not feel like relinquishing this suddenly precious possession. I was tired of being compliant, of being in this beige marriage, of being almost dead to caring about anything. So I said, *I'm keeping the toaster oven.* He was shocked, I think, and called himself to arms. He started arguing that it was his mother who gave it to us, and so, he reasoned, it should be his. I then countered with unthinkable rationale about how much his mother loved me and would miss me in their family. It devolved quickly, as you can probably imagine. He ended up leaving the house for the last time, slamming the door behind him. I watched him drive off. I eyed the toaster oven on the counter and realized that it was a symbol of his mother's love and I would need that in the days ahead. It had served a greater purpose than melting cheese on toast. It was a springboard that propelled me forward with more energy than I had felt in over a year. It allowed me to give voice to good and juicy emotions that had been lying dormant and that, if left unexpressed, might have otherwise morphed into the doldrums. It allowed me to watch him leave our little home, knowing that along with fear of the future, I was now accompanied by a sense of relief that allowed me to breathe and begin again.

Here Come Da Judge

Not everyone gets divorced easily. The dissolution of a marriage, a union of two people with their dreams and intentions, can be a complicated mess of legal maneuvers and emotional land mines. But not mine. My divorce from Danny Weaver was a breeze. We had no money, no accumulation of possessions, no children. We had nothing much to argue over. I liked cats more than he did, so I got Alice. He needed a car to get to New Jersey, so he took the old Honda with 135,000 miles on it. What I valued most about our marriage was his mother, and I figured I could not negotiate for half of her. So off he went into the sunset of academia on the East Coast, and I remained in North Dakota to continue my young life. I was 25.

My parents were never in favor of my marriage; they made that perfectly clear. Danny was from Lawton, Oklahoma. His parents were conservative Republicans, he had a slight Southern accent, and he ate mayonnaise or ketchup on top of most of his food. So when I told them we were getting divorced, they were less than sympathetic. Because they found cagey and oblique ways of saying *I told you so*, I did not consult them about how on earth a person obtains a divorce. I went to them for very little and they returned in kind. So I set about finding a lawyer who might help me navigate the straits of marital termination. Since I had no money to pay the attorney, I was immediately referred to the Legal Aid office in Grand Forks. There, a young female attorney reassured me that the end of my unfledged marriage would be an easy slam dunk.

I signed a bunch of papers and had to send a few copies to Danny (who, by this time, had started his new life in Franklin Park, New

Jersey). I paid her about $25 and in a few weeks, she and I met at the courthouse in what was hilariously called downtown Grand Forks. We sat outside the chambers of Judge Kurt Swenson. My Legal Aid attorney assured me that there would be little discussion, that the marriage would quickly face its grim reaper and that we would be on our way in a matter of minutes. A clerk came and ushered us into Judge Swenson's chambers. There was no one in the room other than the two of us, the judge and a court reporter who sat poised, ready to type into some record the end of the brief marriage of Danny Weaver and me.

On Judge Swenson's desk, which my Legal Aid attorney called a bench, even though it looked absolutely nothing like a bench, was a wooden nameplate, a framed photo of a woman and three children (insensitive, I thought, for a family court judge), and most disturbingly, a fairly large ceramic bobblehead of a judge. It seemed to be staring at me with its jiggly head introducing itself with the byline of: *Here Come da Judge!* Where was I? How did I get myself into this particular situation? I grew up in New York City, smack in the middle of Manhattan, and here I was getting divorced from an Oklahoman (who at that moment was in New Jersey), in front of a judge in Grand Forks, North Dakota — a judge who had a bobblehead likeness of himself on his mahogany desk. What wrong turn had I taken?

I had never been in front of a judge and so, as a first experience, it could have been worse — but it also could have been better. Judge Swenson started out: *Young lady, why are you wanting to end your marriage?* I told him that Danny had moved to New Jersey and I did not want to go with him. I went on to say that we both were at peace with this decision. He proceeded to lecture me about the sanctity of marriage and about the serious mistake I was making. He ended by cautioning me with these words: *Well, young lady, I will grant you a divorce, but let me tell you something: if you ever choose to marry again, follow your husband wherever he goes.*

This took place in 1973. I had gone to a college that was a hotbed of feminist thought and civil rights activism. In the year previous to my divorce, the Equal Rights Amendment was finally passed by Congress, having languished there for close to 50 years. So you could say that I bristled, that I felt hot with rage, that I recognized the position I was in. I had to silence myself, take another one for the team if I wanted to get the hell out of there and be unmarried again. So I nodded, trying to keep tears of anger from rolling down my face.

We left the courthouse and the Legal Aid attorney dropped me at my house. I lay down with Alice, my devoted cat, and cried my heart out. Suddenly, I felt completely alone. I decided to call Danny to tell him we were no longer married. When he answered the phone, I could tell he had forgotten that the court date was that day. I started to cry and told him what the judge had said. Danny was sympathetic, declaring that Judge Swenson was a "male chauvinist pig" and that I should not let him get to me. Instead of thanking me for going through the whole uncomfortable process of dissolving our brief, flat marriage by myself, he asked me if he could call me back the next day. He had to get going; he said he had tickets to a Bob Dylan concert in Manhattan. I was furious. And hurt.

I lay back down with Alice and thought about Danny's mother. If she had known what I had been through at the courthouse while her son was getting ready to go to a Bob Dylan concert, she would have been warm and commiserative. But I knew I could not call her. She did not deserve to be in the bind of loving her son and comforting his now-ex-wife. That was the loss I had to grieve and accept. And I did not call my parents. The story of Judge Swenson and his bobblehead would have only added fuel to their fiery judgment that North Dakota was probably the worst place in the country, maybe in the world. So I lay there alone with my cat, gearing up for the long slog out of the blues.

As divorces go, mine was cheap, quick and uncomplicated. The only wrinkle was the judge. Not following Danny Weaver to New Jersey turned out to be one of the best decisions of my life. I stayed in Grand Forks for another four years, much to my parents' dismay. I met some wonderful people, one of whom I married and lived with until his death 34 years after leaving Grand Forks. I learned so much from my first trial run of a marriage. Never marry anyone for his or her mother or anyone else, for that matter. And always marry someone to whom you feel connected and with whom you have energy and fervor. And if you should need to divorce, don't get scared of the judge. He or she does not know the whole story. But try to find one without a picture of an intact family on the bench and, one would hope, with no bobblehead in sight.

No Dak Black

At the age of 25, I found myself living alone in North Dakota, recently divorced from a nice enough man. Soon after he left town, my cat — Alice — and I moved to a tiny house in Grand Forks closer to the University of North Dakota. The house had been a chicken coop at one time. It had three rooms, all of equal size. The front room was my bedroom and it fit only a bed and dresser. I actually had to sit on the bed cross-legged to open the dresser drawers. The back room was the little kitchen, and the middle room was a living room, of sorts — though you could not really do much living in it. The house did have a basement, though it was dank and inhospitable. It was just right for Alice's litter box.

What the chicken coop house did have was the most wonderful garden space behind the garage. It got full sun and the Red River Valley soil was so rich you could practically hear it asking for seeds. I knew absolutely nothing about gardening, having grown up in New York City where I believed most vegetables came directly from the grocery store. I planted my first garden with the help of friends. After they saw that I had planted some marigolds with the roots up in the air and the flower buds in the soil, they knew I needed help. Eventually I planted a vegetable garden; the corn was so high I could not reach the tops of the plants. And the tomatoes were like huge orbs of juicy sweetness. There was also a tall, mature apple tree next to the garden. In the spring, it was covered in white flowers and when I sat underneath the umbrella of its majestic branches, I thought that maybe this is what heaven was supposed to be like.

I had no money, although my ex-mother-in-law sent me $100 a month for a while. I had several odd jobs that kept a meager flow coming in — at least enough to cover the rent. I applied for food stamps and used those for groceries. But I needed a real job, one with benefits and enough money to not have to worry all the time. I checked the bulletin boards all over the University, where I was taking classes in ceramics. I was in love with throwing pots and was aware that pottery was keeping me sane. I qualified for in-state tuition, so the classes were close to free. And I had a small job in the Ceramics Department, so that helped. But I searched for full-time work constantly.

The *Grand Forks Herald*, the local paper, had job listings in every Sunday edition. I scoured them weekly. One Sunday, I saw a notice of a job opening at the North Dakota Department of Rehabilitation in the Services for the Blind Division. The office was on campus and the job was for a communications instructor, someone to teach recently blinded adults how to read braille and use the abacus as a calculator. The ad said training was provided. I always liked the look of braille; it reminded me of letterpress printing and I thought it was beautiful. So I applied for the job. The man who headed the Division was blind and he had a sighted employee who taught mobility skills. The position I was interviewing for was held by another sighted woman, named Iris, who was moving to another state. I remember thinking how strange it was that she had the same name as the part of the eye chiefly responsible for how much light reaches the retina. It was Iris who interviewed me and eventually offered me the job. It paid very little, but was lots more than what I was used to.

I started training with Iris immediately. I worked with her alone each morning for four hours, and then I sat in on her teaching sessions with clients in the afternoon. She gave me a braillewriter (like a typewriter, but with only nine keys) to take home, along with homework every night. Braille is an amazing system, so economical and particular that you could swoon in amazement.

It takes a lot of concentration to learn. At first I learned it visually, and then after about a year of teaching, I tried to learn it tactilely — which was much harder. Learning braille was so interesting that I forgot I would have to teach it to traumatized adults, people who had only recently lost their vision.

After Iris left town, I started teaching on my own, mostly older adults who had lost their vision due to macular degeneration, diabetic retinopathy and glaucoma. I saw several women in their 70s who were sweet, but not keen on learning what is basically a new language. I did my best with them, mostly listening to stories about their lives. I tried teaching them to use an abacus for calculating numbers, but they had no interest. I feared that they would return home, to their farms or small towns, and just wither away from boredom. I also saw a couple of adult men with albinism who had lost their vision very gradually and were now almost completely blind. One of them had tried to learn braille in high school, but did not have the patience or motivation back then. Now he wanted to be able to read the braille edition of *National Geographic* by himself, so he was impelled to learn. Unfortunately, he had a better attitude than aptitude; braille was hard for him. He liked using the abacus better and figured he would try to get *National Geographic* through Talking Books for the Blind.

And there was a woman in her 50s who had lost her vision after suffering the effects of giant cell arteritis. She was in shock, really, from having a disease that started out with tenderness on her scalp near her temples and resulted in total blindness. At each session she wept and could not concentrate. I think it was while helping her that I decided to go into psychology for my life's career. Learning braille was less significant for her than being heard and understood. She liked the abacus and we played lots of math games on her little calculating tool, adapted with a foam layer to hold the beads in place.

I would have to say that my star student over the two years I worked there was a young man named Tom. He was 21 and came from a small town smack in middle of the state, with a population of well under 1,000 people, literally called Center, North Dakota. Tom's parents owned the town's auto body shop, and Tom worked full time with his father until his eyesight got too bad. He had retinitis pigmentosa, a congenital disease wherein the retina gradually degenerates, and over time the visual field is reduced to a tiny pinhole of light. Tom's disease progressed quickly. He was almost totally blind.

Tom was a stoner. He had smoked pot since he was 12. He talked slowly, in a marijuana drawl, and he dressed like someone who had only occasionally used a washing machine. In today's parlance, he was both grungy and chill. He strolled into the classroom using his cane in an almost choreographed way, whistling or humming. He could have been a disheveled, pothead version of Fred Astaire. He intrigued me. He wanted to learn braille, he said, because he wanted to be able to read the *Bismarck Tribune* as he grew older. That was the paper that printed his grandparents' obituaries — and he figured he would have to write the obits for his own parents when the time came. His goals were not lofty, but rather, utilitarian. He was motivated, and that's what made teaching him braille satisfying and enjoyable. He had a wry sense of humor and used all kinds of weed-related expletives when he mastered something new. He yelled out, *Oh baby ganja!* when he learned the braille shortcut for the letters I-N-G. There is an involved method of using letters for numbers in braille, and when he got the hang of it, he muttered under his breath, *wacky tobacky!* Once, after a long lesson, he said to me that I was a *Maui Wowie* teacher. I was profoundly touched.

The people who came to the Department of Rehabilitation had been referred by their local social service agency. They were usually approved for about of month of training in cane mobility and communication skills. Many of them did not make it through the whole month. They either did not have the lodging they needed for the duration of their stay or they got frustrated and did not stick with the program. Most of them went home on weekends to be with their families. Occasionally the female clients would bring me bread or sweet rolls that they or a family member had made over the weekend. My job was really about being in a relationship with these dear people who were in the process of suffering one of the most profound losses of their lives.

Tom stayed for the entire four weeks. He went home on the weekends and brought back amusing stories of getting high with friends. I had no judgment about this. If he could get joy and pleasure from altering his reality, more power to him. One weekend he reported that his friends had taken him to a quarry outside of Center. They smoked some pot and then swam in the cold, deep groundwater of the gravel pit. He said it was *Rasta canasta*! On the last day of his being my student, after we played a few abacus math games, he said he had a gift for me. He unzipped the front pocket of this backpack and took out a baggie of marijuana. As he reached out to give it to me, he said, *I brought you some killer weed. I grew it myself. I call it No Dak Black.*

I received it warmly; he could not see that I was moved to tears. Tom had handed me some of his joy — an amazing thing, if you think about it. I was only a few years older than Tom, and my life would go on with so many choices and possibilities. He knew he would be in Center, North Dakota, for the rest of his life. He would swim in the gravel pit in the summer, and in the winter he would do some small things around his father's auto body shop. He was hoping to use his abacus to help his father with the books. He now knew braille, however, and had access, not only to the *Bismarck Tribune*, but also to books and magazines, and even to a braille wristwatch. I took my bag of No Dak Black home and shared it with some friends. I told them about Tom and we toasted him. In the bottom of the baggie were some seeds. A few weeks after I said goodbye to Tom, I soaked the seeds for a day or two and then planted them in my garden between the rows of gigantic corn. No one ever saw the plants but me. And they brought a sweet harvest. I cut them down and dried them in the fall and put the crumbled leaves into a small jar, labeling it "No Dak Black." I often wonder how Tom has fared as an adult. I hope he is reading all that he can get his hands on in braille, that he got to write and, most importantly, read his parents' obituaries in the *Bismarck Herald* and that, when he delights in what he is able to do, he still shouts out, *Oh baby ganja!*

One Lucky Widow

Prologue

I won't start with how much I loved Peter. All stories that end with a sad death begin with a description of how much love there was. It's enough to say that my grief is a testament to the love I felt — and still feel. It's not love and connection that perish. What dies is the body, the person, the husband. Death punctuates the progression of a marriage with a period. Yes, of course he lives inside me and in the hearts of our friends; and he is there every time I look into the faces of my children. Yet there is no new shared data in our marital life together starting from the moment he died. Since then, it has been my thoughts and memories of him and of us that have kept me company.

On the days following Peter's death, the house was filled with people from morning until night. Many of them were our closest friends. There were dozens I had never met, people whose lives were touched by Peter and who were stunned by his death. I heard many stories, some of which I had remembered hearing from him, and others that were new. It was not until the house was empty and I was finally in bed, that I began to feel the undertow of my own recollections. No one knew what we had gone through as Peter's health betrayed him. In the dark, each night for months — no, years — I went through the files of recorded memories in my mind, trying to sort, savor, and make sense of our experiences. Some of what I recall is in fragments; some is as linear as a straightedge. A hurricane had struck our family without much warning. The eye of that storm had stalled for 10 years over our little universe, and though we persisted in living the best life we could, it took Peter's life and changed mine forever.

PART ONE

[The Blue Truck]

Before Peter left work at the end of each day, we generally spoke by phone about what we were going to make for dinner or about the kids' activities. Reliably, he got home when he said he would. So it was strange and concerning when, in May 1992, he started arriving home late, sometimes by 45 minutes to an hour. I worried, of course, and greeted him with questions: *Where were you? How come you didn't call? What kept you at school?* He answered with vague explanations that got lost in the chaos of dinnertime with hungry kids. I knew this was a busy time of year, with school breaking for summer vacation in a month. His job was stressful, helping teachers, students and parents negotiate learning and behavior issues in the classroom.

I am not proud admitting this, but I became suspicious. My work as a psychotherapist included hours of listening to couples talking about affairs and betrayals. I had never known Peter to be anything other than trustworthy and loyal, but I began to imagine how easy it would be for the mother of a student to fall for Peter, a kind and sensitive man who was keenly interested in her child. So one night, after the kids were asleep, I asked him if he was having a relationship with anyone, emotional or otherwise. He looked shocked that I would ask this. *You have been late coming home every school night for the last two weeks,* I explained. *Of course, I am wondering why.*

He sighed and looked sheepish as he said he was sorry. He then stood up and took his wallet from the back pocket of his jeans. In it were two small Polaroid photographs of a blue pickup truck. *I've been going to Amigo* [our car repair shop] *every day after school. This 1953 Dodge pickup truck has been on their lot for a month or two. I haven't been able to resist visiting it on my way home from work. It was Todd's family's truck on their farm, before*

*they opened the car repair shop. It's such a beautiful truck — the
stick shift is not on the floor! It's on the column: three on the tree!*

I looked at the pictures and started to laugh. I asked him why he
hadn't told me about his visits to Amigo. He said he felt guilty
for coveting the truck and he just was hoping to get it out of his
system by visiting it. The next morning, I noticed that he had
placed the two Polaroid photos on his dresser, next to framed
pictures of our two children.

At my lunch hour later in the day, I drove to Amigo and talked to
Todd. I told him about Peter's getting home late and how he fessed
up to his after-work dalliances. He said that Peter was smitten by
the truck as he took me around back to see it. It was, indeed, a
beautiful, classic, handsome, utilitarian pickup truck. The shape
of it reminded me of trucks kindergarten kids might draw. And
the shade of blue was heavenly, a cross between navy and azure.
The sweetest details of the truck were the canary yellow wheel
rims. I could almost understand Peter's obsession with it. I then
asked Todd if he would sell it to me so I could give it to Peter for
our 15th wedding anniversary in a couple of weeks. He loved the
idea of Peter's owning the truck and we talked about cost and
made a deal. The next day, I brought Todd a check and he told
me he would keep it on the lot in the same place it had been for
over a month. He agreed to keep it a secret.

On the evening of our anniversary, May 28, we planned to go
out to dinner. I said I wanted to drive to the restaurant so that
the route would include passing Amigo. I turned into their side
lot where the pickup truck waited for him, washed and waxed.
Hanging on the tailgate was a sign I had mounted earlier in the
day. It said: HAPPY ANNIVERSARY, PETER! I LOVE YOU. He
looked stunned. I held out the keys to the truck and said, *It's
yours.*

Peter wept in my arms for at least 10 minutes. And then we
continued on to dinner in Peter's 1953 Dodge pickup truck, the
best gift I would ever give to him.

Chapter 1

Wednesday, September 22, 1999

Our daughter, Emily, is away at college. She's struggling and we're worried about her all the time. We are on edge, even in our sleep. This is the plight of a parent. No one is told at the outset of parenthood that you are embarking on a lifetime of disquietude if your newborn infant grows up and suffers. I think it should be printed on the side of condom wrappers and on the packaging around birth control pills: "Use This Unless You're Ready For A Lifetime Of Worry." Of course, the anxiety is there because you have fallen in love with the baby; you have committed your life to her survival. And when she's not thriving, neither are you.

Peter and I are getting ready for work on this beautiful crisp autumn morning, having had less sleep than we need. I'm going to leave the house in about a half hour to go to my psychotherapy practice. I have eight patients on my schedule today. I need to pack a lunch, so I'm rushing around. Peter's getting out of the shower. He puts on a crisp blue shirt and is looking for his khakis. He's in a hurry to get to work. He has a meeting with the parents of a child who is having trouble at school. Peter is the Director of Guidance and Testing at a private school in Minneapolis. He takes his job as seriously as I take mine.

I notice Peter's legs. He is a very handsome man and looking at him has been a pleasure from the moment I laid eyes on him in 1975. His ankles look different this morning. They look puffy and swollen. So I say to him: *Peter, your ankles look odd, like you have edema.* He looks down at his feet and ankles. Defensively, he says, *No, they don't. They're fine. Look at yours. Your ankles look swollen.* I say again, *I mean it, Peter, something looks off.* He gets irritated with me, so I drop it. I feel distant from him. I don't understand why he's not taking me and his ankles seriously. He puts his socks and pants on in a hurry and goes downstairs to the kitchen. We do not discuss his ankles again for a week.

Chapter 2

Friday, October 15, 1999

It's now Friday night and Peter and I are sitting high up in the bleachers, watching our son, Alex, play junior varsity football. He's a freshman at the same school where Peter works. This October night is chilly, after a beautiful Indian summer day. The leaves are at their peak of autumn splendor and the sight of a high school football game from where we are sitting is like an iconic picture of the Midwest. I decide that perhaps I can get Peter to listen to me as we watch the game. I tell him that I'm worried about something and that I need him to take it seriously. *Your legs look different to me; they seem to be changing shape and they look a little bruised.* He sighs. *Please to go to the doctor to have them looked at.* He says he feels fine. I tell him I'm glad of that, but it seems like the sudden swelling should be checked out. I tell him that edema can be related to problems of the heart or liver or kidneys. He is so wishing I would not be bringing this up. I whisper that I love him and don't want anything to happen to him. He sighs again and says he's fine, but that he will, for my sake, get in to see the doctor next week. I turn and kiss his cheek. I say *thank you* a number of times. We sit together watching the rest of the game with our arms around each other.

When Peter had a medical exam the following week, his blood work revealed that his platelet count was unusually low. His internist noted the edema in his lower legs and sent him to get an EKG and an echocardiogram. These cardiac tests came back normal. After several months of monitoring his platelet count, which never climbed to a higher number, Peter was referred to a hematologist at the University of Minnesota. After several consultations there, it was decided that a bone marrow biopsy was necessary to rule out blood cancers, like leukemias and lymphomas. His ankles remained swollen most of the time.

Chapter 3

Thursday, February 17, 2000

I'm driving Peter to the biopsy appointment on a bleak winter day. Parking at the University is always frustrating, especially with all the high banks of shoveled snow, so I let him out at the entrance of the hospital building. As I walk from the parking lot, being careful not to slip on the ice, I wonder if we're about to enter a life of illness and treatments. The people in the procedure area look sick. Peter, on the other hand, looks good, and seems to be enjoying talking to the doctors and nurses. I'm anxious and scared. Peter is telling the doctor that he would like me to be in the room with him during the biopsy. She tells him this is fine. We enter a room where Peter undresses and gets into a gown. He is asked to lie on his stomach. Two nurses enter the room along with the doctor who will perform the procedure. One nurse gives him an injection of something she says will relax him and help numb the pain of the procedure. The other nurse is monitoring his blood pressure. We are all chatting as the drug begins to work. Then the doctor spreads the gown open in the back and palpates the top of Peter's pelvic bone. She then takes a large syringe with a long needle attached and inserts the needle into Peter's backside. Peter is talking a lot. I'm holding this hand. He sounds almost drunk. The pressure of his bone marrow being sucked into the syringe leads him to say, *I'm in a washing machine. I'm in a washing machine.* All four of us are laughing and I stroke his hair. He's saying how much he loves women. *Women are so much better than men.* He says he's so glad to be surrounded by the wonderful women who are taking care of him in this room. He announces how much he loves me and says my name over and over again. We are all smiling and there is almost a jolly feeling in the room.

A week later we got the results of the bone marrow biopsy. They were clear: no cancers or serious blood diseases. I cried when Peter read me the test results. The question remained however: why was his platelet count low? When doctors can't figure out the cause of an abnormality, they use the word "idiopathic" in the diagnosis. So Peter, who had previously been as healthy as anyone I had ever met, who ate health food long before there was a surge of popular interest in nutrition, who ran and swam, played tennis, and had no bad habits, suddenly had something called idiopathic thrombocytopenic purpura. For some unknown reason, Peter's immune system was producing antibodies that were attaching to his platelets, mistakenly indicating to his spleen that an infection was brewing. So then the spleen, whose job it is to fight infection, was removing too many platelets from Peter's bloodstream. The hematologist said that his platelet count was not dangerously low, so the prescription was for Peter's blood to be monitored frequently. We both thought we had dodged a bullet.

[Peter]

Peter was a strong and energetic 26-year-old when I met him in 1974. He grew up in Palo Alto, California, the third of four children. His father was an endocrinologist and his mother took care of the house and raised the children. His entire family exuded vitality, endurance and hardiness. Despite significant cardiac issues, his father lived actively until the age of 93. His mother faded slowly due to Alzheimer's, yet she survived until she was 94. Peter was the most athletic of his siblings, capable of playing any sport at a high level of performance. His position in the family was defined by his physicality, his generous spirit and his quirkiness. He was the only child who struggled in grade school. He went to Berkeley, while all the others went to Stanford. He was not interested in science or business, as the others were. Instead, he was drawn to history and child development.

I believe I was meant to know him, to love him. My being from New York and his coming from California made North Dakota the unlikeliest place to meet. He came there to study education at a progressive and experimental graduate department started at the University of North Dakota by a Harvard professor. And I got to Grand Forks by way of a starter marriage that ended almost before it began. After that said husband left, I stayed put, not knowing where to take my young life next. I had many small jobs to keep myself and my cats afloat. I discovered ceramics and started throwing pots like a fiend. I thought I might stay and get a Master of Fine Arts, but then I got romantically involved with my ceramics instructor and that was the end of that. After a job teaching braille to recently blinded adults, I decided that psychology was perhaps a better fit. It was in my second year of graduate school that I met Peter. I was invited to join him and a mutual friend for dinner at his house. He lived in a charmingly tired farmhouse on the edge of Grand Forks. He bought it for $7,000, the amount he had inherited from a distant relative. It had three bedrooms and one bathroom. The dining room was the center of the house, with a gigantic heating vent at one end of the floor. Underneath the grate of the vent was a hole in the floor leading to a small wooden staircase down to the scariest basement I had ever seen. The foundation of the house listed terribly, and I could almost see the headline: University Student Found Dead Under Rubble of Collapsed Local Farmhouse.

For dinner, he made curried zucchini soup, a salad and homemade bread. And he talked about a book he was reading and loving. I was spellbound. A man who loved to cook, bake bread and read books? I did not know that one of those existed. I was taken by his kind manner and his love of small children. He was in the process of creating a Head Start nursery school program for the children of migrant workers living in Crookston, Minnesota, across the Red River from Grand Forks. We started seeing each other daily after that dinner. Falling in love with him came easily.

I learned about his gift of excellent coordination early on. I enjoyed playing tennis and was fairly good at it. The first time we played together, I did pretty well — until I learned that he was playing with his nondominant arm. When I watched him play with an evenly matched opponent, I saw a strong and agile athlete moving naturally and competitively across the court. He was an even more striking swimmer. He could swim the crawl for almost an hour in a pool or across a lake. He moved through the water as though he were born there. He was like a fish; I used to tell him he had gills for lungs.

When he was a child, Peter had trouble in the first few years of school because he entered kindergarten a year too early. His family was organized around academic excellence and achievement in all things. Peter's birthday put him on the cusp of being either the youngest in his class or the oldest. His parents erred toward starting him in school at the young end of the spectrum. And by the fifth grade, it caught up with him (and with them), and he was asked to repeat that year. Having to be in the fifth grade twice was humiliating for him, as it would be for most children.

This crisis, at such a young and impressionable age, was the bolus of pain that sparked his curiosity to understand the development of a child's mind and well-being. It was always at the heart of his compassion for children who were having trouble in school. In fact, he developed an expertise in assessing children for academic and emotional readiness for learning. Instead of being trapped by shame, he allowed his experience to guide him to a passion that accompanied him until his death.

Peter was beloved in his workplaces. The other faculty looked to up to him for his expertise in assessing the problems in a classroom, and creating solutions that improved the lives of teachers and children alike. He was gifted in understanding the dynamics between parents and children and between families and schools. Throughout his early career teaching preschool and kindergarten, and as an instructor at the University of Minnesota in Early Childhood Development, Peter understood children and had a connection to them that was grounded in respect, comfort and joy; he not only loved babies, but also adolescents — even the petulant ones. His career ended with his role as a college advisor.

If there is a heaven or some other region of afterlife activity, I'm sure he is nurturing those babies in Limbo and all the children who died too early. He is teaching them to read and to make things out of the clouds. He is, no doubt, helping them to be curious about whatever being dead is like. He would not be able to do otherwise.

Chapter 4

March 2002

Peter is getting ready to have shoulder surgery. Because of his love of old bricks and gardening, he has torn his rotator cuff while creating a beautiful courtyard on the south side of our house. The surgeon has been informed of the platelet problem and his hematologist has cleared him for the surgery.

It goes smoothly with no need for a blood or platelet transfusion. We feel lucky. Peter has been well, without a medical issue for two years. As he is recuperating from surgery, we talk often about how fortunate it is that he is healthy. Intending to take only a week off from work, he has a complication in his healing process and needs to stay home longer. He is complaining about this. He wants to return to his normal, active life. He is not the best patient in the world.

[Bricks]

The name Peter is derived from the Greek word *petros,* which means stone or rock. Perhaps a coincidence or maybe he was just living up to his name, but Peter had an obsession with bricks. He looked for old bricks, pavers and cobblestones in abandoned lots, construction sites, areas where old roads were being excavated and replaced with asphalt. When Peter held an old brick, his hands hugged the red clay and shale rectangular bar the way a person might hold a small animal. And because he only liked old ones, they were like archeological treasures. He collected them, stacked them and used them. He made beautiful garden bed borders out of them as well as two patios, one on the south side of our house and the other at the far end of the lot, hidden by shrubs and trees.

It was on a summer night in 1995 that Peter woke up Alex at midnight. Alex was 12. *Hey, Bud, want to come with me in the truck to get some bricks on Aldrich and Bryant Avenues? You know, where they are tearing up the streets?* I had been asleep, but awakened when I heard the truck's engine below the bedroom windows on the driveway. I got up and saw that Peter had left a note in the bathroom. *Gone to get bricks. Took Alex. Love you.* I looked at the clock. I could not believe what Peter was up to at midnight. I went back to bed.

At 3:15 a.m., I was awakened by the sound of bricks being stacked, a repetitive, clunking hard-rock sound. Peter and Alex tried to be quiet, but they failed miserably. It seemed to me that they had amassed enough pavers and cobblestones to build the next Great Wall. In the morning, Peter brought me a cup of coffee and invited me to come outside to look at his cache. I stood in our driveway still in my nightgown, drinking coffee and listening to Peter tell me how beautiful this neatly organized pile of bricks and cobblestones was. He said that the road construction site was full of brick hounds; he was proud of how Alex fit right in.

Peter spent the rest of the summer washing the bricks, scrubbing each one with a wire brush, stacking them according to size and condition, dreaming of everything he was going to pave and edge.

Chapter 5

Thursday, June 6, 2002

I'm grieving that Alex is about to graduate from high school and leave home. I can't imagine how life will be without him in the house. I'm also deeply proud of him. It's a bittersweet time. Peter is exceptionally busy with the end of the school year. His shoulder is still bothering him. He's taking Vioxx, a strong anti-inflammatory, for the pain. Alex is playing in the Minnesota state tennis tournament. He's in the semifinals this morning, his graduation day. Peter's parents and my mother are visiting from both coasts, and they get to watch him. He wins the match and tomorrow he will play in the finals.

Friday, June 7, 2002

We are at the Northwest Tennis courts in a suburb of Minneapolis, where the state tennis finals are taking place. The matches are played on indoor courts despite the beautiful spring weather we are having. Alex is playing an archrival. There is a palpable tension in the air, a kind that is particular to high school sports. Peter and I are watching from a viewing area above the tennis courts. We are drinking cranberry juice that we have bought from a vending machine. This is the same juice we had the day before. Peter thinks it will bring Alex good luck if we drink the identical thing we drank yesterday when he won in the semifinals. The match is tense. Peter gets another bottle of juice. He leans over and whispers, *Isn't it weird how cranberry juice makes your poop dark?* I look at him and motion that I have not noticed that. I almost forget what he has just said because Alex is winning the match in a tiebreaker. The crowd goes wild. So do we.

Saturday, June 8, 2002

Everyone is tired today. Peter's parents are staying in their motel for much of the day, wanting to rest up before they head back to California. My mother is staying with us. She and I are cooking and talking in the kitchen. Peter is complaining that he feels like he's coming down with a virus. He feels exhausted and a little achy. He's upstairs sleeping. I bring him some dinner on a tray. He has no appetite and eats nothing. His coloring is slightly grayish.

Sunday, June 9, 2002

Peter wakes me up early in the morning and asks me to come downstairs to the bathroom next to the kitchen. He says his bowel movement looks strange. He wants my opinion. I look into the toilet and say, *You need to go to the ER right now.* The blackness of his feces shocks me. And his face is pale, with a greenish tone. He is getting dressed and I call his father at the hotel. His father, a physician, agrees that Peter needs to go to the hospital.

It is 9:00 a.m. and we are in the ER of a local hospital. Because he is bleeding internally, they see him immediately. CT scans are ordered, and blood and platelet transfusions are started. They admit him to a private room on the fourth floor. His father thinks the bleeding is a side effect from taking Vioxx for his shoulder pain. His internist is called and agrees that this is a possibility, though unlikely.

Chapter 6

Thursday, June 13, 2002

After two endoscopies, one colonoscopy, two CT scans, three ultrasounds and four days of blood and platelet transfusions, the doctors at the local hospital tell us that Peter has esophageal varices, enlarged veins in his esophagus that are a symptom of serious liver disease. On the fourth morning at this hospital, Peter is greeted by a nurse who says there is an order for him to have a liver biopsy and she is there to transport him to the procedure area many floors below his room. No one has discussed this with him. Peter refuses to undergo the procedure until he can speak to the gastroenterologist. The nurse replies that once the biopsy results are available, the gastroenterologist will see him. Peter says emphatically that he is refusing the biopsy until he can discuss the risks with a physician. I make two calls: one to his physician brother in California and the other to a friend, a gastroenterologist in Boston. Both of them are adamant that a biopsy should not be performed until a hematologist is consulted. Liver biopsies can result in some bleeding and due to his platelet problem, they recommend having a hematologist weigh in. The nurse calls the physician who is waiting for Peter in the biopsy area. She refuses to come up to Peter's room to discuss the procedure. A "patient advocate" is called. He arrives and listens well to Peter's and my concerns. He is able to get the physician to talk to Peter. When the doctor arrives, Peter asks her if she has read his recent health history in his chart. She says she has not. She has only read the recommendation from the gastroenterologist on duty the day before. Peter asks to see a hematologist. The doctor seems annoyed, but approves his request.

Later that day, a hematologist arrives at Peter's bedside. He has reviewed his entire chart. He states unequivocally that a liver biopsy is too risky a procedure for Peter to undergo. He is getting transfused day and night with both whole blood and platelets and is in no shape to take that risk. This hospital is clearly not a place where Peter wants to continue treatment. I make two more calls, this time to people who I hope can help us enter the Mayo Clinic system immediately. Through some miracle, we get an appointment at 5:00 p.m. with a liver expert at Mayo. Peter discharges himself against medical advice and receives a scolding from the hospitalist on call. We drive straight to Mayo in Rochester, Minnesota, with a quick stop at home for Peter to get some clean clothes and to touch base with our house, which he misses terribly.

We arrive in Rochester at 4:45. The drive is very quiet: Peter is exhausted and I'm scared. I'm driving, of course, and we hold hands most of the way. I barely notice the astoundingly beautiful fields of hay, early corn, and oats. Peter is to see a Dr. Kamath, who turns out to be one of the most soulful, compassionate, competent physicians either of us has ever met. He asks Peter an hour's worth of questions, examines him thoroughly, and then admits him to the hospital a few blocks away. As I hear Peter state his age, 53, I am suddenly aware that he looks older than this, and I feel a new level of anxiety. Peter has signed some release documents at the Minneapolis hospital so that his records can be accessed by Mayo. Dr. Kamath reviews them carefully. He tells Peter that it was an excellent decision to refuse the liver biopsy. He says that there are other ways we can attain useful information about his liver. And some of those tests will be performed in the hospital the following day.

Esophageal varices are the result of blockages in the blood vessels of the liver, particularly due to increased pressure in the portal vein. This is the large vessel that delivers blood to the liver from the spleen, pancreas, intestines and stomach. When this happens, it is usually due to scarring of the liver tissue resulting from cirrhosis or other liver diseases. To avert these blockages, blood flows into much smaller vessels, which are not designed to carry large amounts of blood. This can result in a rupture of the vessels and internal bleeding from the esophageal area in the body, a medical emergency.

The condition of pressure in the portal vein is called portal hypertension. In addition to esophageal varices, other symptoms of portal hypertension can include ascites (an accumulation of fluid in the abdomen), encephalopathy (a brain disorder caused by the liver's inability to clean the blood, resulting in confusion or a change in mood and behavior), and a reduction in the amount of platelets and white blood cells in the blood.

What brought Peter into the hospital in the first place was bleeding from esophageal varices. The procedures that were done at the first hospital ruled out clots or masses in his gastrointestinal system. By the time he met with Dr. Kamath at Mayo, the first order of business was to determine how severe his portal hypertension was, as well as to treat the variceal bleeding in his esophagus. They tried to band each enlarged esophageal varix. He had complications during the procedure and ended up in the ICU, barely able to breath. Once he recovered from that, they tried sclerotherapy, whereby a solution is injected into the bleeding varices — much like what is done in the treatment of varicose veins. Fortunately, that worked.

[The Monterey Peninsula]

Peter's roots were in California, his home state, though he preferred the Midwest. When we visited his parents and siblings in the Bay Area, we would often steal a few days from our time with his family and go to Carmel, on the Monterey Peninsula. His family had friends who lent us their tiny cottage whenever we could use it. It was on a street about five blocks up the hill from the breathtaking Carmel beach.

We had our vacation rituals: we always stopped at Pezzini's artichoke farm in Castroville on the way to Carmel. We stocked up on enough artichokes to have them at every lunch and dinner of our stay. We always walked the dunes at Asilomar and hiked at Point Lobos. My favorite place in the area was China Cove in Point Lobos State Natural Reserve. We would sit on rocks and watch the sea otters playing in the ocean with cormorants, herons and gulls flying overhead. The Monterey cypresses, which line the shore, are perhaps my favorite tree, and Peter took photographs of them every time we were there.

Each morning, we would get up and walk into town and buy the Monterey paper as well as the local Carmel weeklies. We brought them home, made coffee and breakfast, and sat out on the sweet patio flanking the cottage. The local paper had a section called Public Record. We enjoyed reading aloud the police incident reports and the court dispositions. They always made us laugh:

One dog off leash approached and attacked another dog off leash.

Squirrel trapped in house on Ocean Avenue. Owners stayed in motel until it was removed.

Two backpacks lost on Del Mar beach.

Husband and wife got into a heated verbal argument after a day at the beach.

Peter and I loved to read after a day hiking or exploring something new in the area. We would carry chairs and towels, along with our books, down to the astoundingly beautiful white sand Carmel Beach, bordered on the north by Pebble Beach golf links, and on the south by the silhouette of an iconic Frank Lloyd Wright house on Carmel Point. We would read for an hour or two and then take a break, walking the length of the beach. When we got to the north end, Peter always climbed the rocks to look for errant golf balls nestled in the cracks of the cliff. I imagined the fancy golfers overshooting the 18th hole, sending their little white golf balls into the perfect Carmel atmosphere, ready for Peter to collect them and take them back to Minnesota. California golf balls transplanted in the Midwest, just as he had been.

Every evening, we walked down to that same beach to watch the sun set. The image of the cypresses profiled by the magnificent palette of colors in the sky amazed us each night, and those memories are forever engraved in my soul as some of the sweetest times in our marriage.

Chapter 7

Mid-July 2002

Peter is home, having spent eight days in June in the hospital at Mayo. He is mowing the lawn. It's a hot, humid Minnesota summer day, the kind when you perspire just walking to the garage. I'm home from work earlier than usual, Alex is upstairs watching a baseball game on television, and Emily is at her job. I look out the window and am glad to see Peter being active. We know he has something very wrong with his liver and we know he has portal hypertension. However, we don't know what is causing the disease process or even which disease he has. We spend each day and evening together, grateful for all the time we have at home and not in a medical setting. Yet there's an anxiety running underneath everything.

I bring him a glass of water and have to yell above the din of the lawn mower to get his attention. He turns the machine off and drinks the entire glass. I notice that his coloring does not look right again. I tell him what I see. He goes into the house to look at himself in the mirror. He agrees he looks grayish. He insists on finishing the lawn. I say that I think we need to go to the ER. He fights this for about 20 minutes and then relents.

We drive to a different local hospital than the one he went to in June. They admit him and send him to the ICU. He is bleeding internally. I relay all the medical information I can to the doctors there. After many hours and consultation with Mayo, they decide to send him to Rochester by ambulance.

It is 8:00 at night. I go home and pack a bag. Alex, just out of high school, is out with friends, so I call him to say that I'm going to Rochester and will spend the night at a motel across the street from the hospital. I know he is going to ask if I want him to come along, and while I would love his company, I want him to stay in his own life and not be buffeted about by all the medical emergencies of this summer. I leave home at about 9:00 p.m. The drive to Rochester is so dark, both in terms of light and my mood. I'm scared and exhausted. I have been learning as much as I can about liver disease, believing that if I stay ahead of the information given to us about the possibilities of what is causing this internal bleeding, Peter will have a better chance of recovery. I'm aware that this is superstitious, but I keep researching all the types of liver disease associated with portal hypertension anyway.

This was Peter's second bleed. We did not know it then, but Dr. Kamath was keeping track of how many times Peter was admitted with internal bleeding, due to protocols required for surgical treatments. This stint in the hospital included a procedure called a transjugular liver biopsy, whereby a sensor was threaded through Peter's jugular vein to get a more accurate read on the amount of pressure in his portal vein. The procedure had its risks, due to his low platelet count. Because the fluid in his abdomen (ascites) was significant, and because his platelet count was low, a transjugular biopsy of his liver was thought to be safer than a direct liver biopsy through his abdomen. Nothing happened to Peter without complications, it seemed, and this procedure proved to be no different. The measurement for normal portal hypertension is between 3 and 7; Peter's, according to the transjugular test results, was 27. The questions remained: what was wrong with his liver?

Why was his portal vein so compromised, resulting in such dangerously high venous blood pressure? Why was this happening now? Was this a condition that had been brewing for years? Was it related to his swollen ankles of two years ago? I asked so many questions of the doctors, I could tell they were annoyed. I had an almost obsessive need to know, to understand: what was happening to my formerly healthy partner, a man with more energy than most people, a person whose only vice was overworking?

The day following the procedure, Peter remained in the hospital and I went back to Minneapolis to work for several hours before returning to Rochester in the late afternoon. This became my schedule for the week Peter was there. After two days in the hospital, Peter felt pressure in his chest and belly. He had lost his appetite and felt pain when coughing. A hospitalist examined him and said there was fluid in his chest cavity, a condition known as pleural effusion. The fluid had to be removed by a procedure called a thoracentesis. An analysis of the pleural fluid gave more data pointing to a serious liver disease, but which one could not yet be determined.

Chapter 8

End of July 2002

Peter is on the porch of our house, reading. I need to talk to him about many things, including the upcoming move to New York that Emily will be making at the end of August. Alex will also be leaving for college in mid-August. We are a family of moving parts, like most families with emancipating children. What makes ours different is that Peter is going to Mayo at least once a month. He has had two major internal bleeds. And after his last episode in the hospital, we learned that if he has one more, he will undergo a significant surgery. We are attempting to live normally, but there is nothing normal about what might lie ahead. We are wary, keeping our eyes peeled, working hard to be hopeful. There is palpable anxiety in our household and I'm constantly vigilant, watching for changes in his coloring or his appetite, a sudden malaise. He wants to do what he has done always — to muscle forward. He plans on helping Emily with her U-Haul packing in a few weeks. He is getting ready to go back to school for faculty summer workshops. He is gardening, taking care of the lawn, cleaning the garage. He tires more easily than usual, and that makes sense to us since his stints at Mayo take so much out of him.

My education continues in all things concerning the liver. I have always been curious about medicine and the body. My father was a cardiologist and I often sat in his car when he went out on house calls. I loved hearing about what was wrong with his patients. I loved the plastic models of body parts he had in his office: the heart, the kidneys, the liver. And now, so many years later, motivated much more by fear and the dread of loss, I am preparing myself for understanding whatever comes next.

[No and Yes]

While researching liver diseases, I came upon an interesting term, lily-livered. It means faint of heart or lacking fortitude and grit. In medieval times, it was believed that the liver housed courage. A person who lacked courage was said to have no blood in his liver, and thus its color changed to that of a lily. I discovered this on a day I had been thinking about how much work marriage entails — so I said out loud to myself, *marriage is not for the lily-livered*. It is hard work to keep a partnership vital and generative, intimate and reliable. We know conceptually that each person enters a committed relationship with emotionally overstuffed luggage, secret rituals and inclinations, vast regions of cluelessness and an unconscious arsenal of hurtful habits. Yet we are drawn to merging with one another, promising to hang in there through disappointments, poverty, wealth, bad moods, illnesses, incompatibilities, annoyances and various other connubial plagues until death.

Throughout my marriage to Peter, I was almost driven crazy by his tendency to say no before he would say yes.

Gail: *Want to go out to dinner tonight?*
Peter: *No, not really. We have food here.*
> A few minutes later: *OK, yeah, let's go out to dinner.*

Gail: *How about fish tonight?*
Peter: *No, let's have chicken.*
> He goes to the store and comes home with salmon: *fish was a good idea.*

Gail: *I'm going to the farmers market. Want some heirloom tomatoes?*
Peter: *No, that's OK.*
> He calls me on my cell phone: *sure, why don't you pick up some tomatoes.*

Peter: *Does this blue shirt look OK with these pants?*
Gail: *No, not really. The tan one would be better.*
Peter: *No, I want to wear the blue one.*
> Fifteen minutes later, he comes into the kitchen wearing the tan shirt: *I think the tan shirt looks better.*

Of course I brought this pattern to his attention. I pleaded with him. *Could you just practice saying yes first? Change your mind, if you have to, and then say no. But please, for the sake of my mental health, please would you stop saying no before you say yes? And another thing: why do you do this?*

To his credit, he did think about it and tried hard to change the order of his responses to my questions and suggestions. For Peter, this was a deeply ingrained habit. It must have been some vestigial response that worked for him in his family when he was young, sandwiched between his siblings. Off and on throughout our marriage, I watched him trying to reverse his knee-jerk *No*. I could almost see his brain squirming beneath his beautiful head of hair. We laughed about it much of the time, but really it was as annoying to me as my intensity and obsessive curiosity was to him.

As I said, marriage is not for the lily-livered.

Chapter 9

Thursday, August 1, 2002

I'm at my office 20 minutes from home. In between sessions with patients, I check my voice mail. I have a message from Alex, saying to call him immediately. I'm aware that I have a couple sitting in the waiting room, but of course, I return the call. He calmly tells me that he's in the car with Peter and that they are on their way to Mayo in Rochester. Peter's coloring is that grayish green and they are sure he is bleeding internally. I start to cry and Alex tells me that I need to calm down and get in my car and head to Mayo. He is saying that Peter is comfortable in the reclined passenger seat, with a bucket at his feet in case he vomits. I know that Alex is taking on a responsibility much larger than he should at his young age of 18. He's driving his father, a man he so deeply loves, a man who is in such a precarious medical situation, to an emergency room one and a half hours away. Peter wants to go to Mayo, not to a local hospital. Alex, who has been living with the exigencies of the medical traumas this summer, understands his father's desire to be seen at Mayo. I want to protect Alex from the realities of our family's situation, yet I know I cannot. He's firmly embedded in this summer of vigilance, fear and hope.

I take some deep breaths and go into the waiting room to tell the couple that I won't be able to see them. I say that there's a medical emergency I need to deal with and that I will call them to reschedule. I enter the elevator in my building and pray Peter will survive what is next. I get into my car and point it in the direction it knows so well by this time, south on Highway 52 to Rochester. The drive takes no more than an hour and a half, but today it will take over two.

After being on the road about 30 minutes, my cell phone rings. It's Alex who reports a huge accident south of Cannon Falls, midway to Rochester. A semitrailer is overturned on the highway and the State Patrol is diverting traffic onto narrow two-lane roads, bordering expansive farm fields. He says to expect a delay. I feel panicky all of a sudden. I ask Alex to please call 911 and ask for an ambulance to be sent from Mayo so that Peter can get to the hospital as soon as possible. Alex is asking me to calm down. He is saying that Peter is resting comfortably and that my anxiety is upsetting both of them. I feel powerless and indeed, I am. I back off and say that I will see them at the Emergency Room of Saint Mary's Hospital.

After I hang up with Alex, I start to weep. The traffic begins to slow as I enter the diversion area. I feel almost sick with fear. I know I have to surrender to the reality that I cannot change anything about how this day is going to transpire. I turn on the radio and try to distract myself. It is a stunning late summer morning; the sun is bright, with only a few wispy cirrus clouds in the sky. I look out at the beautiful fields of corn and alfalfa and think about how strange life is: so much beauty and so much suffering. I turn east onto a farm road, as the State Patrol is directing all the cars to do. I can almost not believe this is happening. I wonder if this is a parable, some odd allegory I am a part of. The obstacles getting to Mayo today, the day he most needs to be in the hospital, seem almost staged. I make a mental note to remember this morning, no matter what the outcome of the day. I am thinking how odd it is that I grew up in Manhattan and I am now in the middle of the country, practically in the middle of a farm field, chasing after my son and husband to an emergency room 80 miles from our home.

[Gail]

The Midwest was never on anyone's radar when I was growing up in New York City. I knew that Chicago was big, but it never really counted. I knew the Mississippi was a river in the middle of the country, but that was only because it was fun to spell backward. The only place that was of real interest to my parents was New York, Manhattan, the Upper East Side. Maybe Europe got their attention, too. They sent me to a private girls' school and most of the students there planned to go to college on the East Coast. A few of them ended up going to colleges in California, but that was the exception. And maybe a couple went to Northwestern or the University of Wisconsin, but they were almost pitied. The idea of going so far away from the Eastern Seaboard was seen as settling for a Plan B — or maybe C. So when I refused to consider going to college in Massachusetts, it caused quite a stir in my family. I had discovered a small college in Ohio that looked interesting to me. It was outside of Cleveland in a town that bears the college's name: Oberlin. I applied to go there and when I was accepted, I was ecstatic. Not only did it sound like a wonderful college, but also it was the farthest west I had ever been. Everyone, including me, thought Ohio was in the heart of the Midwest. My parents wrung their hands in distress, thinking I was making a terrible mistake.

But it was the opposite of a mistake. It was the best thing that had happened in my young life thus far. I not only got a great education, but I also met people from all over the country. The United States expanded like an accordion. My roommates were from Montana, Texas, Nebraska. I dated someone who grew up in a small town outside Indianapolis. And before I graduated,

I decided to marry my boyfriend, who was from Lawton, Oklahoma. You can imagine the disappointment of my parents.

After four years in Ohio, my new husband from Oklahoma (whose last name was Weaver, believe it or not) and I moved to Washington, D.C. The year was 1970. The Vietnam war was raging and we had been protesting it for most of our college years. I got a job at the National Geographic Society, in their book department. In an act of rebellion against my roots, I took my husband's last name so I became Gail Weaver. We stayed in D.C. for one year and then packed up a U-Haul and drove to Grand Forks, North Dakota, to the school of education there that was attracting national attention. We stayed married for slightly under three years. He was a lovely person, but we were not meant to spend a lifetime together. I stayed on in Grand Forks after he moved to New Jersey (on the East Coast, I want to emphasize) for a doctoral program. I could not stand the idea of moving back in that direction. So I forged my young life in a tiny town in a much-maligned and overlooked state, North Dakota. My parents were distraught, and for some reason my mother sent me a case of Dijon mustard. She felt sure I could not find any mustard in Grand Forks. Of course, mustard is grown on farms surrounding Grand Forks, fields and fields of the most vibrant yellow covering miles of fertile farmland. I knew it was my mother's way of helping me. Dijon mustard — very East Coast.

It was a really good thing I stayed in Grand Forks, because it was there that I met Peter.

After I got divorced, I changed my name back to Hartman, vowing to never give it up again. I figured being called Gail Weaver was more of a protest than I would need from then on. I had fallen in love with North Dakota, with its plains and its simplicity. And I had made good friends there. One of those friends introduced me to Peter. We finished graduate school there and decided to get married before we knew where jobs would take us. I could not imagine getting married in Manhattan, so we went to his side of the country and had our wedding in a grove of gigantic redwood trees outside Mountain View, California. It was a beautiful day, with only our families in attendance. We were married by a warm and thoughtful excommunicated Catholic priest (I am Jewish, Peter was Presbyterian, neither of us observant) with the brilliant California sun shining through the trees. I wore a Mexican wedding dress, and Peter wore a plaid shirt and corduroy pants. And I did not become Gail Clark, remaining true to the vow of never again giving up my name.

Peter and I moved to Minneapolis a month or so after the wedding. He had gotten a job offer from the University of Minnesota, teaching early childhood education. I had visited Minneapolis a few times and loved the feel of the city. We figured it would be a good place for me to look for a job in psychology. He sold the farmhouse in Grand Forks for about four times its original price, and that gave us a down payment on a house in Minneapolis. We gave away our dog, Juneau (a husky that was 40 percent wolf), before we moved to the city. Juneau would have hated the confines of urban life where he would have had no place to run and roam. We wept across the state line as we headed toward Minneapolis, leaving Juneau behind.

If I had not loved being a therapist, I think I could have been happy working for the Minnesota Chamber of Commerce or the Department of Tourism. I walk around, even to this day, with the zealousness of a convert. I have New York woven tightly into my DNA, or maybe New York is just renting a large storage unit in the memory centers of my brain. But I am a Midwestern person at heart. After all, if I include the years I lived in Ohio and take away the one I lived in Washington, D.C., I have lived in the Midwest for 50 years. It's just that every once in a while, the New Yorker in me yells out, *How on earth did you get here?* And that's what happened driving to Rochester that day, following my son and sick husband through fields of corn and alfalfa on our way to the hospital at Mayo.

Chapter 10

Thursday, August 1, 2002 (continued)

I'm incredulous at how long this drive is taking. The farm roads are not running parallel to the highway and I'm trying to stay calm as I take many 90-degree turns. I seem to be going east instead of south. My body is aching with the stiffness that comes from uninterrupted anxiety. I assume, perhaps incorrectly, that most of the cars in front of and behind me are on their way to the Mayo Clinic in Rochester. We are all in the same predicament and what comes to mind is the children's board game Chutes and Ladders. We are all trying to get to square 100. A turn to the east is a chute, a road back to the south, a ladder. I know we will get there. I'm just hoping that Peter is continuing to be conscious and calm. I don't dare call them again.

It is not until 1:00 p.m. that I pull into the parking lot next to the emergency entrance to Mayo's Saint Mary's Hospital. I scan the parking lot for the car Alex was driving. When I find it, I feel weak with nervous relief. I run into the building and ask the woman at the front desk where I should go to find Peter. As I walk down one hall after another, I see Alex standing in front of enormous stainless steel swinging doors. The sign above the door says Emergency. We embrace. I tell him how grateful I am that he kept such a calm attitude the entire drive. I feel his body shaking. He has the space now to discharge all that pent up fear. Peter is being evaluated behind those huge doors. I ask a nurse walking by if we can go in and be with Peter. She is kind and attentive, as she leads us through the doors to a bay marked 4E.

Peter is awake and talking to the doctors who are examining him. There are two nurses checking his blood pressure and attaching an IV line. I lean over the gurney and kiss him on his forehead, his cheeks. He looks pale. He is telling me that Alex is a great ambulance driver and I put my arm around Alex. I keep thinking about how young he is to see all this, to feel all this immediate perturbation. He has always been keenly perceptive, even as a very young child. He is both sensitive and rational, with an even temperament and a wise soul. I can feel him being present and also needing to pull back into his life. He is about to go away to college and needs to keep his feet pointed in that direction. Emily lives in her own apartment in Minneapolis and has a summer job. I am keeping in touch with her by phone.

The emergency room doctors have put a call in to Dr. Kamath, which makes us all feel relieved. As we wait to find out if they will be admitting Peter, the three of us decide that Alex should go back to Minneapolis where he is teaching tennis to elementary-school-age kids at 4:00 p.m. As I walk Alex to his car, we talk a bit before he starts the return drive. I apologize for making his trip to Rochester more stressful with my anxious voice on the phone. I explain that the ambulance idea was a way to make sure Peter would have medical intervention, if needed — as well as a way to relieve Alex of the enormous burden of the drive. He tells me, with the wisdom of someone much older than his years, that we all did the best we knew how and that he was not mad, just scared, too. He laughs as he says that Peter seemed less frightened than the two of us. He describes how Peter was not very talkative on the trip, but when he did speak, he had his sense of humor. He says Peter was completely calm when they came upon the huge semitrailer accident in Cannon Falls. I give Alex a huge hug and ask him to drive safely on his way back home. He says he will and asks me to call or text him when I know anything about Peter. I watch him drive out of the hospital parking lot. I start to cry and yet I know I need to pull myself together before I step back into the intense world inside the hospital.

Chapter 11

Friday, August 2, 2002

I'm waking up in a motel room across the street from Saint Mary's Hospital, where Peter was admitted yesterday. Instead of stopping at a restaurant for coffee, I decide to grab a cup in the hospital cafeteria on my way to his room. I feel the familiar rumbling of anxiety inside me. Since this is Peter's third internal bleed, I'm assuming that today will be when we hear about the surgery he will have to undergo sooner than later. The day is hot and humid, even at 7:00 a.m. August in Minnesota has some sultry days and this is going to be one of them.

Peter is sitting up in bed when I get to his room. He's getting a blood transfusion and fluids in his right arm. I look at him and realize he looks more comfortable than he did in his earlier hospitalizations. I wonder if he is getting used to being a patient. So much can change in a life in a matter of months, days, minutes. I'm aware of how much I love him, how much I want this to all end well and for us to have our old life back when illness was not our primary concern.

A physician is entering the room, flanked by two residents and three medical students. We are more than ready to hear what the verdict is concerning the next step in Peter's care. They tell us that Dr. Kamath wants Peter to stabilize one more day in the hospital, then go home for the weekend to rest. He is to return early on the following Wednesday to undergo a major surgery called a side-to-side portacaval shunt. As they are explaining the surgical procedure, I'm feeling suddenly weak, as though the anxiety has peaked to the point that I need to sit down. I ask the doctor to repeat all that he has described because I want to know as much as I can about what is going to happen when they open up Peter's body. I'm asking so many questions that a couple of the residents look uncomfortable. Peter is not interested in all the medical issues. He wants to get better, to go back to work, to not worry about bleeding. Of course this is what I want, too. I just have that magical thinking gear engaged; if I understand what's happening, then I'm in some control of the outcome. This is such hubris on my part, yet it feels like my only lifeline at the moment.

To repeat, the portal vein carries blood from the esophagus, stomach, intestines, spleen and pancreas to the liver. When something blocks that blood flow, pressure builds up in the portal vein, causing what is called portal hypertension. Peter had significant portal hypertension resulting in his bleeding esophageal varices, fluid in his chest and abdomen, and a reduced number of platelets (which was noted in 1999, and thought, at the time, to be from a problem with his spleen). Another symptom of portal hypertension is called hepatic encephalopathy, which manifests in forgetfulness and mild confusion and a bad breath odor (which smells like a mixture of ammonia and curdled milk). Peter had all these symptoms. Something was impeding blood flow through his portal vein and it was now necessary for him to have this major surgery, whereby his portal vein would be sewn side-to-side to his inferior vena cava, the largest vein in the body and thus one with very low venous blood pressure. The inferior vena cava delivers blood from the lower extremities directly to the right atrium of the heart. Once his portal vein was sewn to his vena cava, blood flow would be diverted around his liver decreasing the portal hypertension and subsequent internal bleeding. Another purpose of the surgery would be to get a look at his liver and to get a tissue sample for biopsy.

Chapter 12

Sunday, August 4, 2002

It is a rainy summer Sunday afternoon, three days before Peter's surgery. I'm lying in bed, exhausted from constant worry and anxiety; a humid breeze is coming through the window. Peter is downstairs talking to a friend who has come over to tell him how to prepare for surgery. Our friend, a physician himself, has had several cardiac surgeries and knows firsthand how to approach the upcoming hospitalization. Peter is taking notes about what foods he should be eating before the he goes in (lots of red meat, among other things, is being recommended). Our friend leaves and Peter joins me on the bed. We talk about Emily's leaving for New York City, Peter's absence from work, and my taking Alex to college by myself in the event that Peter can't make the trip in late August. Peter is making a list of things he wants to do in the next three days. He will call his sister, his parents, his friends at school. He will pack a small suitcase with books and his portable CD player. He will go through his music and choose what he thinks he will want to listen to while he's in the hospital. It occurs to me that he's almost excited, as though this is going to be a vacation. We are lucky to have defense mechanisms. I wish mine would wake up and do their job. I would love to be in denial for a few hours. I'm much too aware of what is ahead, having done a huge amount of research on how the portacaval shunt is performed and what the risks and complications are that come with it.

We fall asleep for an hour or so. When we awaken, the light outside is dimmer, as are our moods. We get up and I make dinner. Alex is home and joins us. I can tell Peter is sad about the possibility of not being able to take him to college in several weeks. He is asking Alex all kinds of questions about his life, his friends, what classes he is registered for.

We are all feeling fear, yet we are manifesting it in different ways. Emily is distracted by her upcoming move to Manhattan, Alex is staying home more than usual, Peter is obsessing about the music he will take with him and I'm not sleeping well. I get up in the middle of the night and go downstairs. I sit on a sofa in the dark and meditate, pray, cry, breathe. I'm dreading the surgery and Alex's going to college. I'm worried about Emily in Manhattan, trying to launch her life in the most unforgiving place I can think of. I'm trying to build compartments in my brain, in my heart, so that I can continue to work, to be a mother and a partner and a holder of medical information.

Chapter 13

Wednesday, August 7, 2002 — 5:00 a.m.

We are waking up in our motel room across the street from a different Mayo hospital, called Methodist. We lie in bed hugging each other. Neither of us wants to get up and face the day. Peter has to check in at 6:30 a.m. Of course, he has not eaten anything for 24 hours and feels jittery, irritable, anxious. I'm using all my energy to not start weeping. It's not the time for that.

The motels in Rochester are set up for sick people. There are signs in the elevators indicating how to get to the lab at the Clinic, or to the hospitals, or to the area where wheelchairs can be rented. There are people in the lobbies who are attached to their IV poles, looking too ill to be out and about. The motel employees all seem trained to be extra helpful. I think of it as a Fisher-Price city, maybe as a Lego toy. The Mayo Clinic Universe set, with doctor and nurse action figures and Lego wheelchairs and gurneys — and a strip of motels with ramps, fully wheelchair-accessible. I tell Peter about this. He puts his arm around me and smiles. He asks me if there is a surgery area in the set where they perform portacaval shunts. I say, *But of course.*

We make our way to the check-in desk at the hospital. There are more people waiting to have surgery than I could have imagined. I'm incredulous that this is happening every day all over the world. People are checking in, lining up, readying themselves to be cut into, to be transplanted, to be reconfigured. Peter and I are being instructed to wait in a room on another floor. We proceed.

We have done nothing but proceed for the last two months: Peter has had seven blood or platelet transfusions, six endocsopies, two colonoscopies, variceal banding, endoscopic sclerotherapy, a transjugular biopsy, a thoracentesis, five hospitalizations, and three internal bleeds. And this all seemed to come out of nowhere. The thrombocytopenic purpura two years ago, with his abnormal platelet count and the sudden edema in his ankles and legs, was most likely the prodromal symptoms of his liver disease. Even on the day of the portacaval shunt surgery, we did not know what was causing the portal hypertension and internal bleeding. Dr. Kamath told us that we would know for sure after the biopsy was performed and sent to pathology. He said Peter was likely to have one of the following: cirrhosis, nonalcoholic steatohepatitis (NASH), or a rare disorder called nodular regenerative hyperplasia. Cirrhosis is a disease in which the tissue of the liver has become fibrotic or scarred and this scarring prevents blood from flowing normally through the portal vein. It can happen in people who do not drink heavily. NASH causes an accumulation of fat, inflammation and fibrotic scar tissue in the liver. And nodular regenerative hyperplasia is a rare disease in which the tissue of the liver is covered with nodules. This happens due to abnormal cell reproduction as a response to injury or inflammation in the vascular system of the liver.

Wednesday, August 7, 2002 — 7:30 a.m.

I'm standing next to Peter, who has been helped onto a gurney in a presurgical area. Two nurses are going to take him to the surgery floor by way of a separate elevator solely serving the surgical patients and staff. He's holding my hand, as the nurses start rolling him onto the elevator, and I bend over and kiss him. I'm not permitted to go beyond the elevator doors. I tell Peter I love him and that I will see him in a few hours. He says something funny and the nurses start to laugh. I'm amazed at his capacity for humor after all that he has been through.

The nurses roll the gurney inside the large elevator, and I'm suddenly feeling weak and almost nauseated. I lean against the cold closed elevators doors and I let out the sobs I have been holding inside for days. A nurse hears me and comes over and puts her arms around me. She leads me to a private waiting area and closes the door, asking me if I would like some tea or coffee. I cannot think about putting anything into my stomach. I sit down and tell this lovely nurse that I have friends who will be coming to be with me midmorning. She gives me a pager and tells me that it will make a buzzing noise if and when the surgical staff wants to communicate with me or when the surgery is over. I'm aware I need to be alone, so I thank her and tell her I will be fine.

I start to cry again, this time quietly. This summer Peter has had such bad health luck, and so I'm fearful that the surgery will result in some terrible complication. I collect myself and decide to call Alex and Emily and some of Peter's family. The room I'm sitting in is too small. I opt to go downstairs, with my beeper in tow, and sit in the waiting area off the lobby. I will call my friends to let them know where they can find me when they arrive in Rochester in a few hours.

August 7, 2002 — afternoon

Peter was in surgery for five hours. He has been in the recovery area for two more. I'm waiting in the hallway outside the room he will be brought to. A few of our friends are with me, not wanting to return to the Twin Cities until they can see Peter with their own eyes. I'm so grateful for their company. I wonder how people go through a health crisis who are alone in the world, or who have poor health care. I'm scared and thankful at the same time. I hear the sound of automatic doors opening close by. A hospital gurney is coming in our direction, accompanied by a three nurses. One of them is pushing the gurney and the other two are helping with several IV poles and monitoring equipment. I suddenly feel weak.

Gail, Gail, oh Gail, Peter says as he opens his eyes. *They opened me up and saw how much I love you.*

The nurses and my friends are smiling. A few start to cry. I tell Peter that I love him, too, and that he made it. *The surgery is behind you!* I say quietly as I lean over to kiss him.

We have to get a gift for Melanie, he says slowly, his speech slightly slurred.

Who is Melanie? I ask.

Melanie is an angel, he replies, his eyes closed. The nurse with his two IV poles adds, *Melanie was his surgical nurse.*

Peter declares, *I love Melanie!* We all smile. I assure him we will find a gift.

[Poems Under the Windshield]

When I met Peter in North Dakota in 1975, I had saved up enough money to buy myself an inexpensive car. It was a maroon Austin Marina; it should have been yellow. It was a total lemon. Peter loved old cars, specifically old Saabs. Really old Saabs that needed tons of work. I called them Saab stories and he called my car Marina Mindfuck. We were both right.

Peter left me little poems that he wrote on torn-off pages from his two-holed-punched daily calendar. I would come out of class and under my windshield wiper would be a poem. Usually it rhymed.

Roses are red
Violets are blue,
I cannot believe
That I have met you.

I dream of you in class
While I sit on my ass
I can't wait to see you soon
Under the sun and the moon.

Will you live with me
Up in a tall tree?
We'll live on nuts and love
And thank the stars above.

Chapter 14

Saturday, August 10, 2002 — 7:00 a.m.

I'm standing in Peter's hospital room, watching him sleep. He's attached to many IV lines. I know he's getting antibiotics, fluids and morphine; there are other bags of fluid I'm unfamiliar with. The surgeon has told us that the portacaval shunt was successfully performed. And Dr. Kamath told us late last night that the biopsy taken during surgery revealed that Peter has a rare liver disease, nodular regenerative hyperplasia. Peter will need to be in the hospital for a week or more. His spirits were high yesterday while the anesthesia was wearing off, and I'm hoping he wakes up today feeling relieved that the surgery is behind him. I'm feeling a combination of exhausted and hyperalert. I feel as though part of me is stuck in the On position, not able to relax or let my guard down.

Nodular regenerative hyperplasia (NRH) is not cirrhosis, but rather another liver disease in which the tissue of the liver is scarred. These scars show up as nodules on and inside the liver, putting pressure on the portal veins. What results is the obstruction of normal blood flow, increased portal hypertension and subsequent variceal hemorrhaging. Since NRH occurs so infrequently, it has not been widely studied, and so there is no known cause for the disease. It is correlated with inflammation and some autoimmune conditions. This was the second idiopathic disease Peter was diagnosed with, the first being thrombocytopenic purpura (ITP). As it turns out the ITP was a result of underlying portal hypertension, though this was not brought to our attention in 2000. We would never have guessed that the edema in Peter's legs and their changing appearance would be associated with a disease of the liver.

Chapter 15

Wednesday, August 14, 2002

Peter has been recovering for seven days in same hospital room. He's in an irritable mood due to his level of pain, which has been difficult to control without IV morphine. Also in the middle of the previous night, he had an episode of something called supraventricular tachycardia. His heart rate skyrocketed to 180 beats a minute. He was rushed to cardiac ICU where they did a procedure that got his heart rate back to normal. I am standing by his bed holding his hand. He is understandably discouraged and says he wants to go home. He is still tethered to many tubes, IVs and machines. He is starting to cry, which I'm thinking is a good thing. A nurse comes in and looks alarmed, asking if anything is wrong. I think, *Oh my God, is anything wrong? Are you insane?* And Peter says, *I can't sleep because of the pain, I'm nauseated from the medications, and when my heart rate spiked in the middle of the night for no apparent reason, I thought I was dying. Other than that, everything is fine.* It's a good sign, I'm thinking, that Peter sounds feisty. It's a sign of energy.

Chapter 16

Saturday, August 17, 2002

I'm at home, excited and anxious. Today Peter is coming home from the hospital. I'm simultaneously preparing for his homecoming and helping Alex pack for college. A friend is transporting Peter this morning from Rochester to Minneapolis, and I'm grateful to not be making that drive today. I feel as though I'm sitting in the neck of an hourglass: I cannot stop time; I feel the inevitability of imminent change. Alex and I will leave at 5:00 a.m. Monday morning for Appleton, Wisconsin, about four and a half hours from home. Peter is both weak and heartbroken; he wants to be able to take his son to college and he will not be able to. He has had a longer stay at the hospital than expected: two full weeks, filled with complications and pain. His recovery, I am fearing, will be an uphill ordeal. He has lost 25 pounds from his already trim frame, he is weakened from the trauma of the surgery and the procedures of the preceding three months, and he has fallen into an understandable depression. He is unfamiliar to himself. He has been, all his life, a person with boundless energy, physically ready for anything.

Through the window I see our friend's car turn into our driveway. I run out and greet Peter, opening the car door and helping him out. I want to hug him, but he is bent over seemingly in a lot of pain. He's asking to lie down as soon as he enters the house. He's nauseated and light-headed. Alex and I get him into bed, helping him to take off his clothes. *I need to get to the bathroom right now*, he says in a low, urgent voice. We help him get there, down the hall. The sounds of his gagging and retching scare me. They are primitive and guttural. Alex is looking concerned and comes over to hug me. I'm having a hard time understanding why he was discharged, still in so much distress. He is moaning in the bathroom, saying that he is scared that the force of his vomiting will tear his incision. I enter the bathroom. He is sitting on the floor, shaking and looking ill. Alex and I help him get up and into the shower. He is weak and holds onto us so that he will not fall. I call Mayo.

Mayo informed me on the phone that Peter had been having difficulty tolerating the oral pain medications, Roxanol and oxycodone. They were making him nauseated. The nurse explained that a medicated patch had been applied to his neck, called a transdermal scopolamine patch. She assured me that this would be helpful to him, that it was commonly used with cancer patients after chemotherapy treatments, and that we needed to be patient. After two more violent episodes in the bathroom, I called Peter's younger brother, an oncologist in California. Take the scopolamine patch off immediately, *he instructed. He said some people experience a pernicious side effect of nausea, vomiting or dizziness with the scopolamine patch, the very symptoms it is prescribed to prevent. I carefully took it off his neck and told him that he would be feeling better in less than an hour. He declared that he was not going to take any more pain medication, so he switched to ibuprofen for the rest of his recovery, preferring postsurgical pain to violent heaving.*

Chapter 17

Monday, August 19, 2002 — 5:30 a.m.

I'm relieved that Peter has been free of nausea since the patch came off. He is depleted of all energy. His appetite is meager and his mood is low. It is feeling almost impossible that this day has come, the day Alex leaves home for college. We have finished packing the cars and will piggyback all the way to Appleton. Alex is in the bedroom with Peter and they are talking. Peter is visibly upset and Alex is embracing him. Less than three months ago, no one would have believed that Peter would be sick and recovering from major, lifesaving surgery — and unable to take his son to college. I have arranged for a friend of Peter's to arrive at the house midmorning so that he is not alone all day. I think he needs the company, and I don't feel secure leaving him alone for such a long span of time. I'm planning to make the return trip late tonight.

Monday, August 19, 2002 — 11:00 p.m.

I have pulled into our driveway and I am sitting in the car, stunned at what the day has entailed. I have been weeping all the way through Wisconsin back to Minnesota. The world feels off its axis: Peter is almost unrecognizable, Emily lives in New York, Alex does not live with us anymore, my role as active parent, changed in a flash. I'm worried about Emily in Manhattan and Peter at home. I need to collect myself. I see a light on in the window of our bedroom. Peter is either waiting up, or has fallen asleep with the light on. Our friend's car is gone, so I know Peter is alone. I'm hesitant to enter the house, to step over the familiar threshold into a different life.

Chapter 18

Thursday, September 26, 2002

It is a golden, Indian summer day. Peter and I are driving to northern Minnesota (I'm behind the wheel) where we are renting a cabin on Lake Superior. We love the North Shore of Lake Superior and Peter has been aching to reclaim a tiny bit of summer. He is strong enough to make the trip (four and a half hours from the Twin Cities), but too weak to pack the car or to drive. We are planning to stay five days, so I'm unloading enough groceries to get us through. The cabin is pleasantly tired and worn — the way we feel. The sound of the lake lapping the shore outside the cabin is heaven. This is what we came for. Lake Superior is a magical body of water, moody, with the grayest-blue water. It is powerful, enormous, dramatic and serene. We need to be out in nature, near wilderness — an antidote to our time at Mayo.

Peter is quiet, as he has been for over a month. He has retreated, like an injured animal, into a region not able to be reached by anyone. He is like a cardboard replica of himself. So we are less interactive than we have ever been. I am trying to read his cues the best I can. I feel lonely, aware that I need to talk about what we have been through, about the trauma we both have experienced. Yet he has a moat of sorts around him. I'm hoping our time up north relaxes him and offers him a better place to heal than the city.

Saturday, September 28, 2002

Peter and I are lying on the smooth boulders outside the cabin. I have spread out towels and brought lots of pillows down to the rocks. It is a comfortable lair, warmed by the slanted sun of late September. We are close to each other, holding hands, kissing each other now and then. *I want to remember this forever,* I think: our respite, the sound of the water against the rocks and even some light spray from the lake, the healing sun, our bodies lying parallel and close. Skin to skin. We are dozing and in my light sleep, I dream that we have washed up to shore, having survived a shipwreck.

[The Recovery]

I would be dishonest if I said that Peter's recovery from the summer of 2002 was any easier than what led up to his surgery. It took three years for him to return to his previous level of energy. His body's thermostat was altered permanently for some reason; he felt cold (or *chilled* as he would say) even on the warmest summer days. His physical symptoms were not as striking as his change in mood. He was cocooned inside a nasty depression for most of this time. It was not a stay-in-bed depression, or even one marked by sleep and appetite changes. He functioned well at work and gave the majority of his energy to the school. Depleted by dinnertime, he would fall asleep early, often while watching a movie on television. At home, he continued to be a cardboard version of himself, with no access to depth or vulnerability, no interest in anything except the mundane surface of living. I spent the next three years in mourning.

My friends and colleagues advised giving Peter time and space to work through the trauma of his health crisis: *don't ask much of him; resist the temptation to engage him in conversation about the summer of 2002.* I admit, I am not very good at restraint over a long period of time. It felt as though I were actively creating an ever-growing elephant in the living room. In fact, the elephant took over the household. In April of 2005, I asked Peter to give me something for my upcoming birthday that would cost him no money: to sit with me on the sofa in the living room and have a conversation about what each of us went through during the months of June, July and August 2002. He said he would think about it.

On the morning of May 4, my birthday, Peter went out and brought home two large coffees, some blueberry muffins and a quart of freshly squeezed orange juice. He arranged this birthday breakfast on a tray and brought it to the living room. We sat together on the sofa, having breakfast and starting what would become almost a full day of talking and weeping, finally connecting after three years. It was like finding someone who was thought to have been missing in action. I felt our marriage reemerging from some foggy netherworld, a purgatory where we were neither here nor there.

I suppose every depression is different from every other, depending on in whom it is residing. Peter's was made of rock, bricks perhaps. Impenetrable. To this day, I think I made an error in not insisting that he converse with me about the events of that frightening summer. I passively colluded with the depression that was creating the rogue elephant in our home. The Birthday Breakthrough, as I called it, was a blessing for both of us. We found a new road that we could traverse together. By the third anniversary of Peter's liver surgery, he had entered therapy with a wonderful therapist to finally work through the unmetabolized trauma he was carrying. And I got my husband back.

Part Two

[Swimming for the Minnesota Twins, 1987]

The Minnesota Twins made it to the World Series, after a less-than-stellar regular season in 1987. The seven-game playoff was against the St. Louis Cardinals of the American League. The home games were played indoors at the Hubert H. Humphrey Metrodome, a large marshmallow-like arena, the first indoor venue for any World Series. Minnesota was impassioned and electric with enthusiasm. People started telling each other about the superstitious rituals they were performing, hoping that the miracle of a win could be ours. The Twins had never won a World Series and we were not expected to win this one either.

Peter was 38 years old, healthy as a horse. He loved to swim long distances. So he decided that if, on every afternoon of a game, he and a friend swam a good distance in Lake Harriet, a city lake near our home, the Twins would win the World Series. Because it was cold in mid-October, they swam in partial wet suits. Someone he knew got him tickets to a couple of the games. He was in heaven. In the seventh and final game, the crowd went berserk in the eighth inning when the final run came in on an RBI double by Dan Gladden. The Twins won the game 4-2 and the Series 4-3. The fans waved their Homer Hankies and cried tears of joy and pride when their Twins, now a team loved like family by the citizens of Minnesota, won their first World Series. Peter believed that, in part, he made it happen. His stamina in the water, his lung power not unlike the gills of fish, contributed to the unlikely win of his beloved baseball team.

Chapter 19

Thursday, February 5, 2009 — morning

Peter has an appointment with our internist this morning. I'm feeling confident about it, since he has been relatively healthy for four years. Checked at Mayo regularly, Peter has had no further bleeds; the portacaval shunt has done its job. His energy has never returned fully, but he has reasonable stamina and his depression has been gone for years. So this morning he is going to get a persistent cough checked out. He has noticed it for a few months and it has not gone away. Both of us assume it's a response to an allergy or a mild asthmatic reaction to exertion.

Thursday, February 5, 2009 — late afternoon

Peter has left me a message at work saying that the chest X-ray looked odd to the doctor and he has arranged for Peter to see a pulmonary specialist tomorrow. I call Peter to ask if the internist said more and Peter says, *Not much. The X-ray showed some darker areas that are probably scar tissue from a pneumonia or bronchitis I had when I was younger.* He is not worried.

Friday, February 6, 2009

It is Friday and I'm home today. Peter is at the office of the pulmonary physician and I'm waiting for his return. Mildly aware of feeling medical anxiety, an emotion I have largely not felt for several years, I look out the bedroom window as I hear the garage door open. Peter is home.

I go downstairs as he enters the house. He is carrying a manila envelope filled with articles and handouts about the diagnosis he was given. He hands me the envelope, telling me that the doctor said only that he has something called pulmonary fibrosis and that he would need to make several appointments with a respiratory therapist. I ask Peter what pulmonary fibrosis is and Peter tells me that he does not know exactly, but his X-ray showed that a lobe of his lungs is scarred. Peter is neither curious nor concerned. I'm suddenly feeling dread and worry, as though plugged into some old familiar outlet of anxious vigilance.

I go straight to the computer and start researching pulmonary fibrosis. What I find makes me feel nauseated and light-headed.

Most cases of pulmonary fibrosis are idiopathic, that is, with no known cause. Idiopathic pulmonary fibrosis (IPF) is one in a category of lung diseases called interstitial. They affect the area and tissue around the air sacs deep in the lung tissue, called the interstitium. In IPF, this tissue becomes scarred, thick and stiff, making it difficult and eventually impossible for the lungs to move oxygen into the bloodstream. It results in the symptoms of breathlessness, a relentless, hacking cough, muscle fatigue, malaise, and clubbing of the fingers and toes. Clubbing is a condition where the digits become rounded, wider than normal, with curved, thick nail beds. IPF has no one way it progresses. Some people remain in stable condition for a long time; others experience a rapid exacerbation of symptoms; and others suffer a stepped-down, gradual deterioration of lung function over time.

IPF patients are urged to use oximeters to monitor their blood oxygen levels and also to participate in pulmonary rehabilitation. Sometimes pharmacologic treatments are suggested, such as the use of corticosteroids (prednisone) to reduce inflammation and a handful of other medications, some of which are experimental, to slow down the scarring process. As the disease progresses, patients almost always have to use supplemental oxygen, sometimes around the clock.

The most extreme treatment for IPF is a lung transplant, for which many patients do not qualify. As with all transplantation, there follows a lifetime of possible rejection and immunosuppressive drugs. The risk of complications within the first year is high, and the survival rates after one year, two years and five years are sobering. Lung and heart transplants are the two most difficult to survive, with lung transplant outcomes far worse than those of heart transplants.

The prognosis: death within three years from diagnosis.

[Magical Thinking]

Peter switched his care immediately to the Mayo Clinic. After a complete examination, Dr. Kamath referred Peter to a pulmonary specialist, Dr. Ulrich Specks. Both doctors assured us that the results of dozens of blood tests showed no connection between the liver disease (nodular regenerative hyperplasia) and the idiopathic pulmonary fibrosis. We drove home after each visit thinking Peter had terrible "health luck." He had to go down to Rochester every three months to have his pulmonary function tested and recorded. Each trip was exhausting. We stopped at a Dairy Queen in Cannon Falls on the way home for an ice cream cone, a small but significant pleasure on those otherwise difficult days. I accompanied him to Mayo each time, not only to be with him, but also to ask the doctor every question I had accumulated from the previous three months of doing my own research.

Admittedly, I was relentless. I learned everything I could online about lung function as well as IPF. From the start, I felt that these two diseases had to be related since both of them had scarring in common. The liver was scarred in such a way that nodules formed in the tissue. The scarring of the lung resulted in a leathery, thickening of the tissue. How could an otherwise healthy man get two separate diseases that caused scarring of major organ tissue? It was too coincidental for my belief system. I was driven to find a connection. Even though I knew Peter was going to die of pulmonary fibrosis, I believed that if I could explain how Peter's liver and lung diseases were related, then magically he would survive. I sat up late night after night at the computer, searching the internet for information that might save his life.

[Two Harsh Realities]

1. After the school year ended in June, when Peter was not distracted by work, he started to wrestle with the realities of the disease. His cough was unabating, but his oxygen levels were still within the normal range. He tired easily, napping every afternoon for an hour or two. Instead of going into a cardboard depression as he did following his liver surgery, Peter became irritable, projecting his anger and resentment outward toward me, the safest person in his life. I was in this for the duration and Peter knew it. He was in the dreaded process of accepting the reality of a terminal illness, one where he was going to gradually lose capacity and capability. While I understood this, I protected myself by telling him in no uncertain terms that he would not be well served by spewing his anger toward me, his closest ally. This did not stop his torrent of criticism, complaints and a threat to get his own apartment. His vitality was starting to wane and he was furious. His words were antagonistic, balking at most of my suggestions, clashing with me regarding the most benign decisions, obstinate, ornery and bitter. His normally calm and even demeanor was replaced by a primitive presence, and even though I understood why he was lashing out, I felt again lonely and misunderstood.

2. In the middle of this already difficult year, my 87-year-old mother began to decline rapidly. She had had two cardiac valve replacements in the fall of 2008, and in June of 2009 she developed an infection in one of the new valves, called bacterial endocarditis. She became critically ill. We traveled back and forth to Long Island to help care for her. My mother adored Peter; in fact, my sister and I used to say that she loved him more than she loved us. So her upset was genuine when she learned about Peter's new diagnosis. She actually did not believe he was sick,

since he was not yet using supplemental oxygen. And this might have been just as well. She died in August 2009 and never had to witness his slow and dramatic decline.

Chapter 20

Wednesday, July 8, 2009

I'm sitting alone on our porch on this sultry evening. The air is muggy, but there is a light breeze, and I'm feeling peaceful. Peter has been in northern Minnesota since Monday and it's a relief to have the house to myself for a week. On the Fourth of July, we had a pivotal conversation that resulted in his agreeing to take a week for himself at his favorite place on earth, the North Shore of Lake Superior. I recommended that he rent a small cabin right on the water and take with him writing materials, books and the CD collection of James Hollis: *Through the Dark Wood: Finding Meaning in the Second Half of Life.* Hollis is my longtime mentor and a writer of such depth, that I know Peter will be changed in some way if he can embrace the wisdom of Hollis's thoughts. There is no cell phone service on the North Shore, so I'm in a state of quiet suspension, absorbing the absence of verbalized strife. I imagine I'm on a beautiful deserted island with rough water all around me.

Chapter 21

Monday, July 13, 2009

Peter returns home from his week alone. He embraces me tightly before he hands me a letter he wrote the night before:

Dear Gail,

I am at a loss for the best way to explain why I have been difficult to live with these past two months. I will try to highlight the reasons I have been so truculent, moody and occasionally mean to you, the person I love most in the universe. Slowly the fog of grief and loss is lifting and more hope and gratitude are bubbling through my body and spirit.

James Hollis has been immensely helpful as I have come to know that the "dark wood" I have been wandering in has all of the "swamplands" he describes: I have been angry, irritable, anxious, pessimistic and depressed. My self-loathing has been splattered, spewed, even flung at you because I haven't been able to "handle" what is happening to me. And being overwhelmed, exhausted and broody has been easier than opening up to self-examination, soul-searching and making needed changes in my interior and exterior lives. Instead, I have forced you to become reactive and enmeshed in my psychic muck. To make matters worse, I expressed (only once) the wish to be left alone, to live alone, while you tried to coax me into rethinking my life in all its facets.

I am so regretful that I doubled your anxiety — of losing me psychologically and physically as well as coping with your mother's disintegrating health. This was enough to flood you with fear of loss and abandonment — squared. Know that I am not going away, but rather coming back home to you as best I can.

I have always believed that I can count on my physical self — to achieve, to be active and to play. In the spring of 2002, starting with my shoulder surgery, the myth of physical invulnerability collapsed. It was only the preamble to tougher, loss-filled events like internal bleeds, procedures, surgery and dark difficult recoveries. In the process, my instincts and my MO took me into darker and darker territories. I felt I had been physically and emotionally sliced and diced into someone I didn't recognize. You could see it growing and eroding, and you tried to help. But I was like a rock, hardened and resistant. For this I am truly sorry and embarrassed.

For these past seven years, my inner gyroscope, compass and navigation systems have been shattered and rendered useless. As Hollis put it, "I was knocked down, hurt, but got up, ready for the next play." I moved forward by focusing mainly on work and productivity; I have been robotic and compromised. As much as I have enjoyed a new role at school, the road to a meaningful daily life will not be found in being a college advisor. If I am able to work for two more years, I will have to adopt a new attitude. Given the latest "curveball" in my health — this interstitial lung disease — I will need to create a more balanced life, less work-driven, more time with the people I love.

My time in cabin #11 has been helpful, restful and inward. If left to my own self-limiting defenses and unrelenting stubbornness, I would not be up here. You gave me a loving kick in the ass, encouraged me to leave the comfort zone of home, and start to reorganize my assumptions, thoughts and behaviors in order to live the best life I can have, as long as it lasts. I am grateful for all your love and constant support. I love you and am coming home with new resolve — to stay open, to work less, to make meditation and exercise a priority as long as I can breathe, to do activities that are restorative, to spend time with friends, and to stop worrying about things that don't deeply matter.

You are my bedrock,
Peter

Chapter 22

Thursday, December 24, 2009

I'm sitting at the computer, having spent hours wrapping Christmas gifts and cooking for tomorrow. For the last 10 months, as Peter has adapted to his limited lung capacity, I have been persistent in digging as deeply as my limited medical knowledge will allow, to find some information regarding a relationship between or a cause of Peter's two diseases. I'm convinced they are related. I have stopped asking questions about this at Mayo, since there is a growing annoyance in their response to me: *Gail* [with emphasis on the hard G], *we have tested Peter for all autoimmune diseases. We can find no connection — which does not mean there is none. But medical science is not advanced enough at this point to give you the information you are seeking.*

It's 10:30 at night and I check my emails one more time before bed. There is one from the husband of a friend of mine, a gastroenterologist in Boston. The subject line is in bold, all caps: **HERE IS YOUR ANSWER.** I open the email and he writes that in the current issue of *The New England Journal of Medicine* there is an article about a study at the National Institutes of Health (NIH) correlating three diseases, two of which are nodular regenerative hyperplasia and idiopathic pulmonary fibrosis. He tells me to pay the $10 required to download it, which I do immediately. I do not go to sleep until 3:00 a.m. It takes me hours to look up all the technical, medical words and to fully understand the significance of the information.

[The Article, The Answer]

At the tips of our chromosomes, there are DNA sequences called telomeres. It was discovered in the mid-1980s that telomeres contain a structure that protects chromosomes from erosion or aging, as well as repairs chromosomes after cell division (mitosis) by way of an enzyme called telomerase. If we had no telomeres, genetically encoded information would be lost each time a cell divides. Three scientists were awarded the Nobel Prize in Physiology or Medicine in 2009, the same year Peter was diagnosed with IPF, for their contribution to science and the world on the critical role of telomeres and telomerase. As our bodies age, the length of our telomeres shortens.

Here was what made this article so significant: it said that telomeres are abnormally short in patients with aplastic anemia, pulmonary fibrosis and nodular regenerative hyperplasia. It is a gene mutation in the telomere/telomerase structure that causes this abnormal shortening and correlates with these three diseases, two of which Peter had. Here was the possible answer to my incessant question: Is there a relationship between Peter's liver and lung diseases, and if so, what is it and what might it tell us about treatment and life expectancy?

This was, all things considered, an article about genetics. I knew nothing of this subject other than what I learned in a basic biology class at college in 1967. So I had to look up hundreds of words and decipher the hieroglyphics of all the charts and diagrams. It was one of the most satisfying articles (on a subject I barely understood) that I have ever read. I felt I had struck gold.

The article was written by two physicians at the NIH, Rodrigo Calado, M.D., Ph.D., and Neal Young, M.D. Dr. Young was the head of the Research Hematology Branch of the National Heart, Lung, and Blood Institute at the NIH. It took me four hours to read and try to understand the article. At 2:30 a.m. I wrote an email to Drs. Calado and Young. It was dated December 25, 2009, Christmas Day. I told them about Peter and his medical history. And I asked if there might be anything the NIH could offer us related to his situation, which might help us going forward. Here is the reply from Dr. Young after the holidays:

Dear Mrs. Hartman:

Thank you for your thoughtful email. It is not wise to opine long distance, but I would agree that a telomere disease would be a unifying diagnosis for your husband.

We have a clinic at NIH that offers second opinions and also protocol treatments. There is no charge for any medical services here as all our patients participate in research. I would recommend your husband visiting us. We can expedite mutation analysis in our own laboratory for him and any other family members who accompany him. Our pulmonary and liver specialists would also be able to consult on his case.

Contact our research nurses Barbara and Olga at 301 402 0764 for an appointment.

NS Young, MD

Chapter 23

Wednesday, April 14, 2010

I'm sitting in a chair in a small, but quiet hotel room in Bethesda, Maryland, a few blocks from the NIH. I'm watching Peter sleep. He has completed three days of blood draws (27 vials), an excruciating bone marrow biopsy with no anesthetic medication, appointments with three hematologists, two pulmonary physicians and two liver experts, and a consultation about clinical trials. His exhaustion on our way back to the hotel last night was palpable. We went to the hotel coffee shop and he ate a sandwich and said he thought he was going to fall asleep at the table. We went straight to our room; I helped him take off his clothes, and he was asleep by 7:00 p.m. It is now 7:00 a.m., 12 hours later. He is sound asleep.

I feel both tired and alert, satisfied and distraught. I have been vigilant, doggedly persistent and relentless in my pursuit of an explanation; amazingly, this trip may well have answered all my questions. But the facts remain: there is neither a cure for Peter's lung disease nor any clinical trials he qualifies for at the moment.

[The NIH]

We were taken to the NIH by van from the hotel on Monday, April 12. We were frisked before we entered the building, in addition to having to go through a scanner. There were rules we had to follow: no phones allowed, driver's licenses had to be left with an official at the reception desk, and we were instructed to wear NIH identification tags around our necks at all times.

Every appointment during the three days started out with the same disclaimer:

We are so sorry that you are ill. We want you to understand we are not a typical hospital with the mission of curing your disease. We are here to do research. If there is a clinical trial that is appropriate for you, we will do everything we can to get you into it. We appreciate your allowing us to gather information about your medical history and your willingness to participate in our research.

The halls of the Heart, Lung, and Blood Institute at the NIH were filled with the sickest people I had ever seen. In comparison, the Mayo Clinic seemed like a wellness hospital. Children were transported in bed-like wagons, looking so frail and lifeless, it made me cry. I saw a young man sitting on a bench — his skin was a shade of dark orange. People on stretchers and in wheelchairs were the norm. This was the end of the line for everyone. All that was left to hope for was an appropriate clinical trial that might offer more days to live or, in everyone's wildest dreams, a cure for their diseases.

The last appointment on Wednesday was in Dr. Young's office. The walls were covered with framed articles and awards, given to Dr. Young over his career. He and Dr. Calado explained to us that it was likely Peter had a particular telomere/telomerase mutation that had caused both his liver and lung diseases — as well as the idiopathic thrombocytopenic purpura (ITP) back in 2000. They would be contacting us as soon as they had the results of the extensive genetic testing. There was one possible clinical trial down the line that Peter might qualify for. Dr. Calado said it was not likely to open up for several months to a year. It entailed taking a form of androgen, the male sex hormone. Dr. Young smiled at Peter and asked how he had enjoyed his adolescence. After some man-to-man sexual innuendos about puberty, Dr. Young explained that androgen seems to slow down the shortening of the telomeres. Peter said he would be interested.

Chapter 24

Monday, May 3, 2010

I am sitting in the parking lot of Trader Joe's in Minneapolis. It is one of those spring days where everything looks new and bursting with life. My cell phone rings. The area code on the caller ID is from Maryland. Dr. Calado is on the other end of the line and asks if I have a moment. He proceeds to tell me that some of the test results are in: Peter's telomeres are much shorter than they should be, indicating that he has a mutation. His telomeres are the length of those of a 92-year-old man. Peter is 61.

Tuesday, June 8, 2010

We receive a letter from Dr. Young saying that Peter has a "novel telomerase mutation called a TERT V170L in the GQ motif." He explains that this mutation, called an autosomal dominant gene mutation, is likely the reason Peter has nodular scarring in his liver and fibrotic scarring in his lungs. The definitive answer to my question.

In the TERT mutation, the mutated gene is a dominant one, located on one of the nonsex chromosomes (called autosomes). A child needs only one mutated gene to be affected by the TERT mutation and subsequent diseases. What this means for us is that Emily and Alex each have a 50-50 chance of having inherited this mutation. It also means that other people in Peter's family might have it. One of Peter's parents no doubt carries the mutation.

Chapter 25

Friday, July 9, 2010

Alex, Peter and I are staying in a quaint log cabin overlooking Lake Superior. Emily is living in Chicago and cannot take time off from her job to join us. We arrived here two days ago and have settled into a restful and relaxing routine of sleeping, eating, taking walks, napping and reading. All three of us are engrossed in different books of the Millennium series by Stieg Larsson. We are having a great time talking about the characters and the intrigue of the stories. I'm taking many pictures of Peter — reading, sleeping, making a campfire, climbing on the rocks; many of them include Alex. I am making a large effort to be hopeful and not pessimistic. Alex is wonderful company. The restorative power of Lake Superior is having a lovely effect on all of us. Even me.

Saturday, July 24, 2010

I am home alone. Peter is driving to Door County in Wisconsin with Emily, who has joined him from Chicago. Peter has planned the trip, renting a cottage on a bay somewhere north of Egg Harbor. Neither of them has been to Door County and they are looking forward to spending some good time together.

Emily calls me in the afternoon, the second day of their trip. She's upset, shocked at Peter's fatigue and demeanor. She has not seen him often during the last year and is now experiencing his limitations for the first time. *He takes two or three naps a day! He's irritable and preoccupied! Something seems different about his personality! Mom, what is happening?* We talk for almost an hour. I explain that oxygen deprivation is hard on his muscles, his heart and his brain. This is the first time Peter's illness and situation have become real to her. I am hoping the two of them find the space and energy to talk.

[Death Books]

There must be as many ways to face impending death as there are words for snowflakes in Alaska. When Peter received the fatal diagnosis of IPF in 2009, he was resistant, in denial, hopeful, looking for ways to distract himself. Then he got furious. And after that, numb. Eventually, he was able to look straight into the eyes of reality, and he started reading everything he could about death, mortality and dying.

He took the following books to Arizona in 2011 on our mandated winter exodus:

> *A Grief Observed* by C.S. Lewis
>
> *The Tibetan Book of the Dead*
>
> *Dying Well* by Ira Byock
>
> *The Denial of Death* by Ernest Becker

Being with Dying by Joan Halifax

How We Die by Sherwin Nuland

Japanese Death Poems: Written by Zen Monks and Haiku Poets on the Brink of Death

A Year to Live by Stephen Levine

Living in the Face of Death: The Tibetan Tradition by Glenn Mullin

Peter kept these books stacked one on top of the other on his nightstand in our small rented cottage in Tucson. Every week the young woman who cleaned it, covered the stack of books about death with a white bath towel. She told us that she could not look at them; they made her too sad.

Chapter 26

Monday, August 9, 2010

We are at Mayo. Peter's pulmonary doctor, Dr. Ulrich Specks, has received the results of the NIH testing. After we finish talking about the mutation, Dr. Specks says that the results of today's lung function tests are not as good as they have been in the past. He tells us in a firm but gentle tone of voice that Peter will need to start using supplemental oxygen. We have been dreading this prescription for a year and a half. We will need to have oxygen tanks delivered to our home on a weekly basis, and Peter will have to wear a cannula in his nose, looped behind his ears, tethered to a portable oxygenator for the rest of his life. I'm choking back tears and am aware of my wanting to get up and leave the room. Peter is stunned.

Dr. Specks goes on, delivering even worse news. He is recommending that Peter stop working. He is saying that schools are petri dishes for bacterial and viral infections. He explains that getting a cold or a flu could cause "acute exacerbation of IPF," a sudden acceleration of the disease process followed by a high likelihood of death. Peter's identity, in large part, has been a person who works with children in a school. His workplace, once a generative space, is now a hazard to his survival.

Dr. Specks is rolling his chair forward to be closer to Peter. He speaks slowly as he states that if Peter wants to do any traveling, he needs to do it soon — and only to places with major hospitals nearby.

In shock, we drive home with a prescription for oxygen and instructions for Peter to retire immediately. We don't stop for a Dairy Queen. We are silent most of the drive, other than my making several calls regarding long-term disability and how to apply for it.

Chapter 27

Friday, August 27, 2010

It is noon on a Friday. Peter and I are home waiting for the first delivery of oxygen. A truck is pulling up with big red letters on the side saying *Lincare, Home Oxygen and Respiratory Services*. I am feeling almost frantic. I do not want this truck in our driveway. Peter is in a chair in the living room, waiting patiently. When I open the front door, there is a large man dressed in a green uniform with *Loren* embroidered on his shirt, standing with two 4-foot blue tanks of oxygen on a dolly. The tanks are covered with decals portraying fire, prohibiting smoking and proclaiming its contents as explosive if heated. Loren asks if this is the home of Peter Clark. I say, *Yes* and hold the door open as he brings these frightening new ballistic-looking tanks into the living room. Peter becomes talkative, actually connecting with Loren. I feel irritable and short. I know Loren is not the problem; he is just the person delivering the oxygen. I cannot help feeling that from now on, we will never again be able to deny Peter's impending death or have hope that he will miraculously recover. Loren does not seem to know how horrible this day is.

They are talking about the Twins and the Vikings, and I interrupt, asking where these tanks should be placed. Loren is recommending one upstairs and one downstairs. I look at Peter and say that I cannot bear to have a tank in our living or dining room. Peter asks Loren if they can both be placed upstairs in our guest bedroom. I mutter under my breath that they are unwanted guests. Loren proceeds up the stairs, saying that if we change our minds about their placement, he can move them when he comes to pick up the used tanks and deliver new ones every week to 10 days. In my brain, I am screaming: *Get these blue tanks out of our house. This cannot be happening. It's an intrusion. I hate them, I hate Loren, I hate the truck in the driveway. I hate this disease. Where did our familiar life go?*

Chapter 28

Tuesday, November 2, 2010 — morning

This is our second day at the Lung Transplant Program at Mayo. Since the progression of Peter's IPF is accelerating, the only hope for prolonging his life is a double lung transplant. We are here to learn about what this would entail and about the statistics regarding complications and survival. Peter spent the entire day yesterday going through a variety of assessments and tests to determine if he would qualify to enter their program. We are now spending several hours talking to a transplant surgeon named Dr. Scott. He is both warm and honest. He has consulted with both Drs. Kamath and Specks, and he is telling us that it would be possible but complicated to perform a double lung transplant on Peter; his liver disease and his portacaval shunt are important factors to consider.

Dr. Scott is explaining that for as many months as it would take to find an organ match, Peter would have to be within 90 minutes of Rochester at all times. He would need to carry with him a special phone, designated to be used only with the Transplant Program. If a suitable organ is found, we would need to live in Rochester for four to six months postsurgery. The complication and survival rates: less than 50 percent of lung transplant patients are alive in five years. He would start taking eight to twelve medications daily for the rest of his life, including immunosuppressant, antirejection, antibacterial, antifungal and antiviral drugs, and he would be on a strict diet, void of many foods he most enjoys. He would not be permitted to garden ever again; gardening, working in the dirt, is one of his passions. He would be at risk, for however long he lives, of organ rejection and infection. He would need to wear a respiratory mask at all times in crowded places. And Dr. Scott adds that we would have to get our cats declawed.

Tuesday, November 2, 2010 — evening

It is 9:00 p.m. and we are in bed talking. The last two days have been emotionally exhausting. We have spent hours discussing the pros and cons of lung transplantation. Peter rearranges the tubing of his cannula and rolls over toward me. He says he does not want to go ahead with the transplant possibility. He wants to live out his life the best he can, knowing he will never recover from IPF. He says he does not want to live in a world of side effects and fears of infection, rejection, limitations — possibly worse than the ones he lives with now. At least for the time being, he says, we can travel to someplace warm in the winter and he can visit the kids in their respective cities. He is free to eat whatever he wants and, if he's alive in the summer, he declares he will spend time gardening. We fall asleep in one another's arms, sad but with less anxiety than we have felt in days.

Chapter 29

Wednesday, November 17, 2010

It is Peter's 62nd birthday. Emily, who now lives in Chicago, and Alex, who lives in Milwaukee, have come home to be with Peter on this day. We are all trying hard to have a good time. We go out to a Vietnamese restaurant that Peter loves. We are on edge. This is the first time Emily has seen Peter with his portable oxygen apparatus in tow. He looks old. Tired. Breathing is getting more difficult. He is no longer working. He spends his time reading books about dying, Buddhism, books by James Hollis and John O'Donohue. He listens to music and he stays in touch with his family and friends by phone. He is trying not to catch a cold.

We keep the dinner conversation light, but I can feel everyone's sadness. Emily is intermittently funny and sarcastic. I know she is wrestling with her emotions, not wanting to reveal her upset. We get through dinner. We return home and Peter gets into bed and we all watch a movie together. There is laughter and a few moments when we all forget what is happening.

The next day, Peter and I explain to both our adult children the nature of the mutation. We tell them that they each have a 50 percent chance of having inherited it. It is their choice to be tested or not. They ask questions about testing: *What would we do with the results? If we have the mutation, will we definitely get these diseases? If we have children, will they have the same chance of inheriting the mutations? Would knowing the information hurt*

us emotionally? Would it prevent us from getting health insurance?
All great questions, none of which we could answer with much confidence. Peter and I spend the next few days knowing we have burdened them with a reality they are as unprepared for as we are.

Chapter 30

Wednesday, December 15, 2010

We are in the office of Dr. Jim Leatherman at Hennepin County Medical Center in Minneapolis. Peter has, at the recommendation of the doctors at Mayo, switched his care to this pulmonary department closer to home. Given that Peter is not interested in a lung transplant, there is no longer a need for him to make the frequents trips to Rochester. He has known Jim Leatherman as a school parent; Jim's daughters were in Peter's class many years ago. Jim looks genuinely sad that Peter has this disease. He is honored, he says, to help Peter at this juncture. We feel held, cared for, known.

Peter and I go out to lunch and talk about the trips he wants to take in the coming months. Starting at the end of December, he plans on visiting his younger brother, Bruce, in Marin County, California. While out there, he will make a trip south to see his parents, both in their 90s. They live in a graduated care facility in Portola Valley, outside of Palo Alto. His father's health is always fragile, but he remains fairly active. His mother suffers from Alzheimer's and no longer recognizes anyone other than her husband. Peter's sister lives in the area, but she will be out of town.

Peter has been advised to get out of Minnesota during the worst of the winter. The cold air worsens his cough. We have rented a cottage on a pecan farm in Tucson, Arizona, for this coming February and March. Peter is telling me this afternoon that he wants to drive to Tucson by way of Austin, Texas, where his older brother, David, lives. He wants to leave in mid-January, in his Prius, packed with portable oxygen tanks and oxygenator and the books he wants to read during the winter. He wants to make the drive alone, and then have me fly down to Tucson when he arrives there on February 10 or so. He has thought about this carefully. After I leave Tucson, he plans to drive through Arizona toward Southern California and then north, up the coast of his home state and on toward Oregon. He then plans to turn east and make his way home through Idaho and Montana. He's planning to visit friends and relatives along the way. He estimates he will be back in Minnesota by mid-April. I'm admiring his perseverance in the face of failing health. I'm sitting across the table from him filled with love and respect.

[Peter's Road Trip, 2011]

In hindsight, I believe the road trip was about saying goodbye to everyone and to the parts of the country he loved deeply. He saw friends, students, colleagues, distant relatives as well as close ones. He stopped in San Diego, Carlsbad, Santa Barbara, Carmel, Palo Alto, Menlo Park, San Francisco; Eugene and Portland, Oregon; Idaho Falls; Butte and Billings, Montana; Bismarck and Grand Forks, North Dakota. He left Tucson on March 11 and returned home on April 10.

He called me every day, sometimes two and three times. He was having the time of this life. He had his portable oxygenator on the back seat, and he got the tanks refilled whenever he needed to at locations he had researched before he left. He loved his Prius and reported with pride how little gas it was using. When he pulled into the driveway on April 10, I had a big banner hung on the garage door saying *Welcome Home*; he got out of the car and we wept in each other's arms. It had been an important journey.

He brought me all kinds of found gifts from his trip: driftwood branches, heart-shaped rocks, shells, agates, several small-town newspapers that he found interesting or funny, a tumbleweed, and a jar of wild huckleberry jam. He was elated to be home, and also exhausted. He took a long hot shower and got right into bed, exclaiming how good it was to be back home.

Chapter 31

Wednesday, May 11, 2011

We are in our dining room with a social worker from the Palliative Care Department of the hospital. When a patient has a fatal disease and has run out of treatments, the program sends a nurse or social worker to the home to help the patient fill out a detailed health care directive. Our social worker has been here for two hours, educating us about all things dire: CPR, life-sustaining and comfort measures (such as pain medication management and food and liquid offered by mouth), hospice care preferences, DNR instructions, wishes for burial, cremation, body donation, preferred music to be played if unconscious. The questions and the information are daunting, at the same time fascinating. I am thinking that there should be a current life directive, some document to be filled out when we are healthy, helping us to discern our values and express important intentions while we are alive. It seems shortsighted that we are not encouraged to think about a meaningful life until we start planning for it to end.

[The Last Wedding Anniversary]

For our 34th wedding anniversary, we went to Carmel, a place we visited many times during our marriage. It was, in fact, where we spent a week immediately following our wedding on May 28, 1977. We even stayed in the same cottage. I can hardly describe the bittersweetness of this trip. Everything we did, every place we went, reeked of sadness, impending death and widowhood. Peter was better than I at rising above the emotional miasma. He bought us a bottle of champagne for the evening. And he went out in the afternoon, oxygen in tow, to buy me two dozen roses. We exchanged cards. I wept. I tried not to, but it was a lost cause. I felt like I was living in a kind of poignancy hell, with no escape, no denial. My heart could barely stand it.

We ate artichokes and shrimp and drank some of the champagne. Peter's perpetual cough and his ever-present oxygenator seemed louder than they had ever been. I could not tune them out. I felt trapped between our years of shared history and our impending separation. Never having been good at hiding how I feel, my enthusiasm for the evening was waning. I regret to this day that I was not able to rise above the sad reality in the service of honoring what was a solidly good, real, honest, brave relationship. We fell asleep in tears, the roses looking on in commiseration.

Chapter 32

July 2011

Peter is spending much of this month outside, lying on his side, slowly and methodically making a stone pathway between the garage and the back garden. When we moved into this house 19 years ago, there was a walkway in this spot made of thin sheets of shale, which soon became shale dust. All that time, Peter has wanted to make a new, improved, beautiful passageway into the gardens he loves.

He is placing smooth blue river rock on top of a sand bed he has created. His oxygenator is on the grass and the cannula tubing is fully extended. The shape of the path is like an asymmetrical hourglass, and the rocks look as though they are flowing, each one laid down with great intention. It is such a beautiful addition to our home. And he is enjoying this project as much as anything he has done in months.

[A Memory from 2002]

On the night before the portacaval shunt surgery at Mayo in 2002, Peter called Carolyn, the sibling to whom he felt closest. She was the last person he spoke to before he went to sleep that night. He told her how scared and tired he was. He explained the surgery and why he needed it. They both cried.

The day after the surgery, when Peter was still in the throes of anesthesia and morphine drips, he asked me if Carolyn had called. I told him no, explaining that I sent an email to his entire family reporting the medical news of the previous 24 hours. I had heard nothing from his siblings. Peter asked every day for over a week, *Did you hear from Carolyn?* I told him the truth, *No.* When he was discharged (more than two weeks after the day of surgery), one of the first things he did, when he could sit up without too much nausea, was to call Carolyn. They had an emotional conversation, one I'm not sure he ever got over. She claimed she had been backpacking in Northern California and had no cell phone service for two days after the surgery. Peter was incredulous. I heard him asking: *You didn't think to find a ranger and use a satellite phone? You didn't think to answer Gail's email, which you received after your trip?* He felt forgotten, insignificant. This experience with Carolyn brought on a torrent of emotion, feeling so little coming from his family at a time of extreme physical and mental vulnerability.

Carolyn did make one visit to Minnesota. It was during 2010, the year he started using supplemental oxygen, eight years after the liver surgery. It was a difficult visit, not because she and Peter argued, but because he did not feel she understood or acknowledged the reality of his fatal disease. There was laughing, joking around, with an occasional oblique slip from one or the other of them. Mostly, it was light. No one was up for rocking the boat until we were actually on a sea vessel a year later, in the middle of the San Francisco Bay.

Chapter 33

Tuesday, October 11, 2011

I am on a boat in San Francisco Bay with Peter, our children and all of Peter's siblings and their families. It is a stunning sunny day, not a cloud in the sky. The Golden Gate Bridge looms like a gateway to some foreign place, its size reminding all of us of our tiny places in this vast universe. We are honoring William Clark, Peter's father, who died at age 93 on July 30. The plan is for Peter's sister, Carolyn, a Zen Buddhist priest, to lead the family through a Buddhist/humanistic/Presbyterian/Quaker ritual, ending with the scattering of Bill's ashes at sea. I'm standing at the bow of the boat, holding onto a railing; I'm observing more than participating. I never felt close to Peter's parents, though they were good, decent people. We were cut from different cloths. I was the bull in the china shop, while they were more like the porcelain teacups. What we had in common was a love for Peter, and that was enough. We had years of congenial connection at family gatherings, but we certainly did not know one another well.

Emily and Alex come over to me to say that Peter is acting strangely. He's making obliquely snide remarks about parity, about why Carolyn is taking charge of the ceremony on the boat and the dinner planned for tomorrow tonight, as well as the impending talk with the family's attorney. He has been more sensitive to slights, to unfair divisions of family heirlooms, to feeling left out. All the resentments he has stored deep in the recesses of his psyche are fomenting a rebellion. He cannot help himself from making wisecracks or from showing displeasure on his face. I go over and sit next to him on a seat near where the anchors, tackle and life jackets are stored. I put my arm around him and give him a kiss. I whisper in his ear: *We will be home in two days. It's going to be OK.* He starts to cry quietly. His cannula is not fully engaged in his nose. He looks disheveled and miserable. His sister begins to lead us in a meditation. Peter turns to me and whispers that he is so angry with her. I hold his hand and look down in my lap hoping he will follow suit. The word *mutiny* comes to mind, and I decide I'm being too dramatic. Surely he will settle down. This is extremely uncharacteristic of him. I'm thinking it's either some split-off piece of grief regarding his father or … perhaps it's his disease. Is his brain changing due to the lack of oxygen? I need to pay attention to this in the coming weeks and months.

The next day, the entire family, other than Peter's mother, is in Menlo Park in the upstairs of a French restaurant called Chantilly. It's a place the Clarks go to commemorate events: birthdays, anniversaries, graduations. And now we are all here, in a reserved room with tables set up in a large square, to honor the life of the family's patriarch. Carolyn has orchestrated the evening. We are having cocktails and Peter is walking around the tables looking at the place cards. He wants to reposition some of them, saying he does not care for how Carolyn has planned the seating arrangement. I see her across the room watching Peter. She looks upset. I tell Peter that maybe he should talk to her first. Peter is saying, *No way. This is the whole family's gathering, not hers. We are all chipping in to pay for this dinner honoring Dad and I will sit where I want to.* For the second time this weekend, Peter is uncharacteristically short-tempered. Carolyn comes over and asks Peter what he is doing. Peter looks her in the eye and responds dispassionately, *I am changing some of the place cards.* Carolyn walks quickly out of the room. Her husband, Billy, is in the hallway and she bursts into tears in his arms.

Carolyn and Peter do not talk again this evening. I know Peter feels hurt by Carolyn, who has shown relatively little concern for his well-being over the past nine years. That, coupled with her possessiveness regarding some family keepsakes, has contributed to Peter's feeling marginalized, embittered and hurt.

At night, Peter cannot sleep. He's restless and is perseverating about the place cards. He's saying that Carolyn always has gotten what she wants. I rub his back, hoping I can help him get back to sleep. I have never seen Peter worked up like this in the middle of the night. I ask him to take a blood oxygen reading with his oximeter. He says he's fine. I ask him again, *For me, please just put the oximeter on your finger.* He does it and his reading is on the low side of normal. He turns up the oxygen level on his portable oxygenator.

[Choosing a Cemetery Plot]

It was on a beautiful fall day in late October 2011 that Alex was visiting from Milwaukee. Peter asked him if he would have any interest in coming to the cemetery with us to see two possible gravesites we were trying to decide between. Peter and I had been to Lakewood Cemetery several times over the last two weeks. When you buy a plot, you have to work with someone, like a real estate agent. The woman assigned to us, Linda, was a little on the strange end of things. She was completely enthusiastic about these little eternal resting places. I was fascinated with how she talked about graves, urns, headstones and crypts. She seemed to love her job.

Alex said he would like to join us, so off we went to Lakewood Cemetery on a spectacular autumn day. The first possible gravesite was in their *Garden of Serenity*. This is an area near the small lake inside Lakewood, where all the plots are for "cremains." It is a very symmetrical piece of land; the plots are fanned out in even rows with beautiful garden plantings all around and lovely benches placed thoughtfully. There are no headstones here; all the markers are flat on the ground. The closer to the lake's edge, the more expensive the plots. When Linda told us this, Peter actually said, *Location, location, location.* Naturally, he thought a spot farthest from the lake, next to the road, would be fine. Less expensive. When we arrived with Alex, he wandered around the *Garden of Serenity,* reading the markers and looking at the lake and the surrounding trees. He wandered up to the row closest to the lake and said, *Here. I think a plot here would be good. It has a nice grassy space next to it, where I could come and spread out a blanket and have a picnic next to you.* Peter was so reactive to the probable price tag, that he did not even hear the sweet sentiment in Alex's preference. Peter responded, *No, that's ridiculous. It will cost a fortune. That's a waste of money!* I interrupted, offering to call Linda from my cell phone. *Linda, it's Gail Hartman. Say, I am standing in the* Garden of Serenity *with Peter and our son, Alex, and we are wondering about the price of the grave, number 43G.* Linda looked it up, and said, $12,500. I thanked her and reported the news to Peter and Alex. Peter went nuts. *That is highway robbery, an insane price tag for a hole in the ground.* And then Alex put his arm around Peter's neck, and said, *Dad, this is not like reserving a permanent parking spot downtown. This is about eternity.* Even Peter had to laugh.

We then went over to the other side of the lake where the second possible gravesite was. This one was under a lovely maple tree and not far from the lake. It was a flat grave, though some of its neighbors had headstones and granite benches. It was a mixed section of the cemetery, cremains intermingled with casket burial sites. Alex liked it immediately. He said, *This is like where we live in the city. The* Garden of Serenity *is like the suburbs.* Again we laughed, and Peter was extra delighted because it was a third of the price.

Chapter 34

Saturday, December 24, 2011

It is Christmas Eve. Emily and Alex are home for the holiday weekend. Underneath the attempts to keep things jolly, there is a palpable sense of dread and sadness. We all know privately that this will probably be Peter's last Christmas. What gift do you give someone who will most likely die within the year? I had racked my brain. I decided on a gift certificate for two massages with a wonderful massage therapist he had gone to several times. His body was so sore, muscles wound taut from three years of coughing. But Peter has no intention of using the certificates. He asks me if I want to use them. I tell him that they are for him, that a massage or two might bring him some comfort. He says they cost too much money. This is nothing new, Peter's frugal tendencies. I'm thinking how sad this is — he cannot allow himself this small pleasure, in a time of such distress.

We are telling the kids about our plan to spend much of the winter in Santa Barbara. I thought it would be great for Peter to be near the ocean, rather than at the desert surrounding Tucson. I have reserved a rental house a block from the beach, south of Santa Barbara by a mile or two. Online, the pictures look beautiful. Naturally he is worried about how much it costs. I tell him *We have saved for a rainy day, Peter. This is our rainy day. You will get to be by the ocean for over two months. There are two extra bedrooms, so your family can visit, if you like. And the kids can come out, too.* We will speak to our financial advisor about this, to try to help Peter feel comfortable with this expenditure.

Peter is to leave on the morning of Saturday, January 21, 2012. He will be flying to San Francisco to see his brother for two days. Then he is planning to take a commuter flight south to Santa Barbara where I will meet him and where we will start our winter by the ocean. We have prearranged oxygen delivery. And, at the advice of Peter's physician, we have contacted a pulmonary specialist at a local hospital in the event Peter suddenly declines.

Chapter 35

Saturday, December 31, 2011 — 9 p.m.

We never stay up until midnight on New Year's Eve, but we usually make it well past 9:00 p.m. We are watching a movie together, but Peter has fallen asleep. I'm turning off the television and quietly going downstairs to sit in the living room in the dark. I need to think. I'm lonely, in a way that I can barely let myself know about. Peter is still alive, but he's changing. Sometimes he's almost unfamiliar to me. He's on prednisone all the time, and even on a small dose he seems off, discrepant from the man I have known for over 35 years. I am thinking it's not just this medication. It's the lack of oxygen to his organs and tissues, a condition called hypoxia. I'm reading about this on my cell phone during the last hours of 2011. I go upstairs and crawl into bed. I cannot fall asleep. The sounds from the oxygenator and his coughing are keeping me awake, like a bad lullaby.

Chapter 36

Wednesday, January 18, 2012 — morning

It's Emily's 33rd birthday. She's in Chicago and Peter and I call her first thing in the morning to wish her a happy birthday. Peter has a cold. He is to leave for California on Saturday, three days from now, so he is going to see his doctor later this morning to make sure he can leave as scheduled. I receive a message from him later in the afternoon when I'm at work saying that Dr. Leatherman has prescribed some extra cough medicine and some over-the-counter cold remedies to keep him more comfortable on the flight. When he travels, Peter always wears a medical face mask. He's at the pharmacy picking up his medications and an extra box of sterile masks. He texts me from there, asking if I need anything. I reply that I don't and then add that I hope he can go home and nap the rest of the afternoon.

Wednesday, January 18, 2012 — evening

Alex is taking off from Chicago to go to Germany to visit an old friend living there. This is the first vacation he has taken in over a year. He calls us from O'Hare to say goodbye. Peter is congested and coughing more than usual. Alex is telling him to delay the trip to California in order to get well. Peter says he will think about that and assures Alex that he will make a good decision.

I tell Peter that I'm thinking it would be wise for us to sleep in separate bedrooms tonight. I explain that if I catch his cold, I will not be able to help him. He agrees and says he will sleep in the guest room, nearer to the oxygen tanks. I help get him settled. I sit on the side of his bed and kiss his forehead. I tell him to sleep as long as he can. We talk a few minutes about the kids, hoping that Emily had a good birthday evening with friends, and that Alex is safely on his way to Europe. We talk about Saturday and his plans to visit his brother Bruce in Northern California.

Chapter 37

Thursday, January 19, 2012

8:00 a.m.

I enter the room where Peter has spent the night. He's lying in bed, awake, tears on his cheeks. He tells me that his oxygen level plummeted in the middle of the night. He was able to get enough supplemental oxygen to feel stable, but he is afraid. I say to him that we need to call Dr. Leatherman's office. He agrees. As I go to the phone, he tries to stand up. He's dizzy and unsteady; his oxygen levels are falling again. I help him to the bathroom. He's out of breath. I'm holding the phone, talking to the nurse, as Peter sits on the toilet panting. The nurse is coaching me on how to help Peter catch his breath. *Pretend you're blowing out a candle, Peter. Short easy blows.* He is starting to breathe more easily. I tell Peter that we need to go to the hospital. He is whispering that he does not want to go by ambulance. He says he wants to shower. I'm scared helping him step over the edge of the bathtub. I hold onto him as he stands under the hot water. He tries unsuccessfully to wash his hair. I climb into the shower to wash it for him, as he holds onto a grab bar with one hand and me with the other.

I call a friend and say I need her to come over. I help Peter get dressed and as soon as my friend arrives, she and I support his weight as he goes down the stairs. It takes him 15 minutes to go 14 steps. His oxygen falls at each step and we then wait until he catches his breath enough to make the journey down one more step. I'm thinking we need an ambulance. I say this quietly. Peter blurts out, *No, no ambulance.*

11:00 a.m.

Peter is reclining in the passenger seat of my car. My friend and I somehow got him out of the house, dressed warmly, and into the car. This has taken over two hours. I'm driving to Hennepin County Medical Center where a nurse will meet us with a wheelchair. Peter's eyes are closed. All his energy and concentration are on breathing. I have the heat in the car turned up as high as it will go, fearing that if the cold January air causes him to start coughing, he might choke.

As I pull up to the entrance of the hospital, I notice that my gas tank is on empty. After the nurse and I get Peter out of the car and into the wheelchair, I tell her I need to go get gas and then park the car. She tells me that they will be hooking Peter up to a more powerful oxygenator and for me to meet them in Dr. Leatherman's office.

11:30 a.m.

I'm driving to a Mobil gas station nearby. My mouth is dry; my own breathing is shallow. Adrenaline has propelled me to this moment and I'm feeling shaky as I fill the car with gas. I decide to call Emily in Chicago. She doesn't answer so I leave a message, telling her that Peter is in the hospital, having difficulty breathing — all related to his cold. I tell her I will keep her informed as the day progresses. I try calling Alex, and realize he's on a plane from Paris to Hamburg in Germany. I leave a message.

4:00 p.m.

Peter is in a private room on the fourth floor of the hospital. He's connected to an even larger oxygenator, requiring a mask over this nose and mouth. Even though his oxygen levels are stabilized, he's struggling to breathe and talk simultaneously.

The room is large — the hospital bed looks out onto an urban landscape: an old red brick church across the street with an enormous cross on its roof, and in the distance, the Metrodome, the marshmallow-look-alike stadium for the Minnesota Twins and Vikings. Peter removes the mask and says hoarsely: *Religion or baseball? I think I'll choose baseball.* A cheerful nurse has entered the room to ask Peter what he would like for dinner. With one eye open, he looks at her and says, *What do you have that's organic?* She laughs and says, *In your dreams, Peter.*

7:00 p.m.

Jim Leatherman comes into the room and stands close to Peter's bed. He's here to tell us the results of a CT scan that was done earlier in the afternoon. He reports that Peter's lungs are extremely inflamed. This may be due to an infection, so he will start Peter on several IV antibiotics, as well as a high dose of prednisone. Peter's voice is weak and he can only keep one eye open, but he manages to say he does not want to take prednisone. *I am not a nice person on that drug.* We all laugh, and Jim continues, telling him that the nurses have seen everything, and that he can behave any way he needs to. He explains to Peter that it is critical to reduce the inflammation as soon as possible. Peter asks Jim if there is any chance he can go to California on Saturday, the day after tomorrow. Jim says this is highly unlikely. Sadness and resignation cover Peter's face. Jim goes on to explain that Peter has either an infection, which may respond to antibiotics, or that he has the beginning of the critical condition called "acute exacerbation of IPF." Jim says that we will know more in the morning.

Jim continues talking to Peter about his recommendations. He asks Peter for his permission to be temporarily intubated if the need arises. Peter is trying hard to consider the pros and cons of this — his advanced heath care directive specifies no intubation to save his life. Jim emphasizes that this would be a temporary measure. With one eye open, Peter talks through the decision with me and Jim, and finally agrees. Before Jim leaves his bedside, Peter says, *I have one caveat to my agreement: you cannot intubate me during the San Francisco 49ers game on Sunday.*

Chapter 38

Friday, January 20, 2012

8:00 a.m.

Peter's room this morning is quiet, luminous with oblique winter sunlight. He is sleeping. He has asked me to bring him his red plaid pajamas and a book (*Let Your Life Speak* by Parker Palmer) and I have them in a bag. I take a seat next to the bed. I'm watching his breathing and thinking about all the calls I need to make: canceling Peter's flight to California, his family, our kids, our friends. I'm thinking we may make it to Santa Barbara, albeit later than the first of February. I'm assuming that Peter will recover and then need to rest for several weeks before making the trip.

Peter is stirring. He opens his eyes and sees me. I hold his hand carefully and squeeze it, not wanting to disturb his IV. I stand up and kiss his forehead, the only part of his face not covered by a breathing mask. I tell him how much I love him and he takes off the mask to kiss me. He feels warm and I ask how his night was. He says he had trouble breathing in the middle of the night and called for the nurses. They got him connected to another oxygenator. He's feeling exhausted, weak and achy.

3:00 p.m.

Despite his discomfort and difficulty breathing, he is having a wonderful visit with his closest friend from work, Frank, who stays for about an hour. Frank is telling Peter stories about students Peter has great fondness for. They talk until Peter is unable to stay awake. After Frank leaves, I whisper to Peter that I will be going home to take a nap and will return early in the evening with some food. He squeezes my hand and tells me how much he loves me.

6:00 p.m.

The phone rings at home; it's Jim Leatherman. He asks how I am doing, and I report that I'm hopeful, but anxious. He tells me he just checked in on Peter and has found him stable. Jim gives me his cell phone number, saying I can reach him any time. He is planning to leave town early in the morning for his cabin in Wisconsin, an hour east of Minneapolis. He reassures me he has cell phone service there, and if anything were to change regarding Peter's status, the hospital or I can reach him and he will return to the city.

8:15 p.m.

HCMC is an excellent county hospital and a Level 1 Adult and Pediatric Trauma Center. It is committed to providing care for low-income, underserved, vulnerable populations. Since it is after 8:00 p.m., no one is permitted into the hospital without showing identification to a police officer sitting behind a bulletproof, plexiglass wall in the entryway of the main building. I'm standing in line with about six people ahead of me. Many of them are angry. Either they do not have necessary identification or they resent having to display it. There is a woman ahead of me with a baby stroller, filled not only with a baby, but also with clothes, food and newspapers. She is yelling at a man who is farther ahead of her in line. She yells, *I don't fucking care what you do, just get me into the hospital.* The man's voice is loud as he screams at the policeman that he does not have any identification. The police officer looks nonplussed. This must happen all the time. The police officer motions for me to step forward toward him. I feel so white, so privileged. I want to disappear. Apologize. And yet, I want to see Peter as soon as possible. I get cleared to enter the lobby. There is one tall man on the elevator, dressed in a hospital gown, complete with a blue hospital admission wristband. He looks wildly medicated. I feel scared for a minute, and then relax, remembering the time I worked on a psychiatric unit. He looks at me and says: *I have a hot date on 6C! She's waiting for me and we're gonna paint the town purple!* I reply, *I have a hot date, too, on 4D!* The elevator reaches the fourth floor and I wish him a great night. He laughs and says, as the door is closing, *You better believe it, I will!*

8:30 p.m.

I'm entering Peter's room with spring rolls he wanted from a Thai restaurant in our neighborhood. An older man from Respiratory Services is in the room replacing a monitor on his oxygenator. Peter is talking to him, again with one eye open, asking how long he has been at this job. The man says, *Forty years.* Peter asks, *What did oxygen concentrators look like 40 years ago?* I am incredulous. Peter is so sick and is still interested in this person's life and in history.

I help Peter sit upright enough to eat the spring roll. He finishes half of one, and says he does not have the energy to eat more. I clean up his tray and wash my hands. He falls back to sleep. I'm feeling strangely calm. I look out the windows at the night sky. It occurs to me that every day and night of each year, there are people in hospitals, struggling to breathe. I vow to myself to always remember this.

10:00 p.m.

I'm lying on the hospital bed with Peter. We are having an amazing conversation, one I did not anticipate. I'm saying to him that if he does not survive what we're hoping is pneumonia, his death might be more peaceful than other possible scenarios in the future. He is telling me how much he has to live for: he wants more time for us, he wants to see more of what's unfolding in the lives of Emily and Alex, he wants to listen to more music, and he wants one more summer to watch the garden grow. I look right at him and say, *Fight with everything you have to overcome this infection, but please remember that if the infection can't be overcome, a kind death may well follow.* I don't know what is making me say this. He thanks me, saying he does not know what he would do without me. He says he will think about all of this as he goes to sleep. I get up and kiss him before I leave the room. Halfway down the hall, I realize that I have forgotten my cell phone. I go back to get it and as I'm saying goodnight again, I remember a question I had been meaning to ask him, one of a practical nature. *One of the cats threw up on the upstairs carpet. What magic solution of spot removers do you use to remove the stain?* With one eye open, he says, *I haven't taught you that yet?* And he goes on in a raspy, almost gasping voice, to describe in great detail what I will need to do to take care of this. I kiss him again and tell him I will see him in the morning.

10:15 p.m.

I get on the elevator and press the button marked *Lobby.* There is a old woman on the elevator, dressed in a hospital gown. She looks more medicated than my male elevator companion earlier in the evening. She starts to laugh and exclaims: *What a night! I mean what — a — night!* I look at her right in the eye and agree, *What — a — night! It was a night to remember!* And she squeals, *One for the history books!* I smile as I get off the elevator. I make my way to the front doors of the hospital, zip up my parka and enter the cold, dark night.

Chapter 39

Saturday, January 21, 2012

5:40 a.m.

I'm awakened from a deep sleep by a ringing telephone. I turn on the light and answer my cell phone, which is lying next to my bed. It's a doctor from HCMC. He is saying that Peter had a very difficult night due to his oxygen levels plummeting to 40 percent. They transferred him to the ICU where he could be monitored more closely. Peter is unstable and the doctor is telling me to get to the hospital as soon as possible. I'm standing up. My heart is pounding. I'm pulling on my underwear and pants. I go to the bathroom and then the phone rings again. It's the doctor saying that they have stabilized him with IV Ativan, a medication used to calm anxiety. He says I do not need to break any traffic laws to get there. *Just get here when you can.*

My plan had been to get up at 7:00 a.m. and bring Peter some coffee or tea. I thought I would spend the day in his hospital room, so I have a book and some magazines at the back door, ready for me to put in the car. Instead, I'm rushing around to find a warm hat and scarf. I get into the car without coffee or my reading material. I have my phone in my pocket.

7:00 a.m.

I'm at the ICU desk on the fourth floor of HCMC. I thought the doctor told me to go to a different floor so I have been lost in a maze of critical care units. I have been walking so fast that I'm out of breath. I say to the nurse at the desk, *Peter Clark?* She smiles and points to a room directly across from where I'm standing. I turn around and see Peter through the glass wall of the room. He is sleeping, propped up at about a 45-degree angle on the gurney. He looks peaceful and almost healthy. There are two nurses standing in the doorway, one of them is updating the other about Peter's status. I interrupt and say that I'm Peter's wife. They smile and tell me he is finally settled with the help of some medications. I stare at the digital displays of all his vital signs and say, *Wow, his oxygen level is good!* At that exact moment, all the numbers on the console start to plummet. The nurses move quickly around his bed and one of them pushes a button and speaks loudly, *Code blue, code blue!* I am watching her say this and hearing it at the same time over a loudspeaker. I take one step toward the bed and suddenly doctors and nurses are filling the room. One of them, at the foot of the bed, is looking at the digital readouts and then at me, as he says urgently, *We're losing him. We're losing him. CPR?* Calmly, I look at the doctor and say, *No.* Then Peter dies, before my eyes, as in slow motion, his head tilting slightly to the left, his lips parted, his mouth open. There is no distress. His skin coloring is good.

I'm in shock. The room is quiet, no one is moving. I hear a woman's voice say slowly and softly, *Time of death, 7:04.*

7:10 a.m.

A tall woman has her arms around me. She introduces herself and tells me she is an ICU physician. She says, *I'm so sorry that you have lost your husband, and I want you to know that I have never seen someone make such a good, calm decision regarding CPR in my time on an Intensive Care Unit.* I tell her that both Peter and I had learned about the risks of CPR and I knew Peter would not have wanted to survive in the condition he was in. I explain that he had been suffering for a long time. She says, *You did the most loving thing.*

The room is full of people. I feel frozen, as though time has stopped. The doctor who asked me for permission to perform CPR comes over and hugs me. He asks if we have children who need to be called. He tells me that Jim Leatherman has been notified and is in transit to the hospital. I look at my cell phone. I know I have to start to make calls: Emily, Alex, his brother, my sister, our friends. There are many lovely nurses and doctors taking care of me. They get me a chair. Peter is dead, in the bed next to me. He looks calm, except for his open mouth. His nails look less clubbed for some reason. He is remarkably beautiful. I'm now shaking. This is real. He has died.

8:05 a.m.

Jim Leatherman enters the room. I stand up and we embrace. He sits down next to me and tells me how much he loved Peter. *It was such an honor to take care of him. Twenty years ago, Peter taught my wife and me how to parent. I am so sorry he got this blasted disease.* I ask him if he thinks Peter suffered an acute exacerbation of IPF symptoms and he says he does. He touches Peter's foot on top of the blanket, and I am holding Peter's hand. It is still warm. I begin to sob, as I lean over his body. Our marriage will have no new shared experiences from this moment onward. I am a widow. Our children have lost their father. I will never hear his voice again. He and I have been preparing for this moment for years. From now on, I will grieve for him and for our life together without the solace and gift of his company.

PART THREE

Chapter 40

Patient Belongings

After staying with Peter's body for five hours, several friends drove me to the mortuary where Peter's body would be delivered that afternoon. I signed papers and wrote a check, not fully understanding what I was doing. I trusted my friends. The face of the sympathetic man at the mortuary reminded me of a breed of dog, perhaps a basset hound or a beagle. He had permanently dolorous eyes. He explained the order of things regarding Peter's dead body. The hospital would transfer him to their morgue many floors below the ICU. Then the mortuary would pick him up and take him to their refrigerated storage area across town. In three days, Lakewood Cemetery would go to the mortuary and bring his body to its crematorium.

After our time at the mortuary, my friends took me home. They accompanied me into the house, carrying two white plastic bags from the hospital filled with Peter's belongings. They placed the bags on the floor, next to the living room couch. The printing on the bags said: *Patient Belongings*. I sat down on a chair and stared at the white bags; I was thinking the word Patient was an adjective. These belongings have been patient. *Patient Belongings*.

The house was quiet. Our two cats wandered downstairs to rub against my legs. I told them Peter had died and I started to cry. The phone rang and it was Emily. She was sobbing on the other end of the phone, telling me she was too upset to get on a plane that night. She told me that friends were coming to bring her dinner and keep her company. I was grateful to know she would not be alone. The next morning she would take a flight to

Minneapolis. Alex was in transit, returning from Hamburg by way of Paris.

The doorbell rang, as it would continue to for the rest of the day and into the evening. Many kind people came to share their sorrow, bringing food and flowers. There were a few neighbors, several people from Peter's school, some colleagues of mine, and many wonderful friends. I felt the buoyancy of the crowd, yet I was constantly aware of the bags marked *Patient Belongings*; someone had moved them into a corner. I decided to carry them upstairs to our bedroom. They looked inappropriate in the living room. What could be more intimate than the belongings of a dead person?

As the crowd dissipated, a couple of my close friends suggested that they stay overnight. *We think you shouldn't be alone tonight, Gail.* I knew they meant well and were generous with their offer, but I told them that I was fine being home alone, and would actually prefer it. The kids were coming home in the morning, a close friend was en route from her vacation in Hawaii, another was on her way from Boston, and my sister would be arriving from Baltimore. I would be surrounded soon enough. A psychiatrist friend of mine suggested that I take some Ambien to sleep. She placed a vial of them on the counter. I told her I didn't want to take them, and she insisted I keep them, *just in case.*

When everyone left, I wandered around downstairs. *Where did all this food come from in just one afternoon and evening?* I made sure the doors were locked. I noticed that my friends had parked my car in the garage. *How did that happen without my knowing it?* I realized I was slightly dazed.

Upstairs, I changed into my nightgown. I sat on the bed next to the two white plastic bags filled with Peter's things. I was scared to look inside, even though I knew each item would be as familiar as anything I owned. Slowly, I untied the cinched bags.

From the first one, I unpacked his blue jeans, his T-shirt, his belt, his wallet, his glasses, the book by Parker Palmer, the oximeter, his plaid pajamas, his underwear and his cell phone. The second bag contained his worn L.L. Bean brown jacket, his striped blue wool hat, some gloves and a box of hospital Kleenex. At the very bottom of the bag was a tiny can of hospital apple juice.

Peter could not be dead because his clothes still smelled of him. Maybe this was a dream, a trial run, a dress rehearsal. I was watching myself get into my side of the bed. I turned over, toward where his body had been for over 35 years. My cats jumped up on the bed next to me. I wondered if they thought he was on his way to Santa Barbara — which had been the plan on that day. I told myself to remember to call the travel agent to cancel our flights and our three-month rental by the ocean. Our house had never felt this quiet. I heard myself breathing for what seemed like the first time in many years. Peter's coughing had been the nocturnal din to which I had adapted.

The tiny can of apple juice was on the dresser and I could see it from the bed. He never had a chance to drink it. I started thinking of so many things he would not be experiencing, starting at 7:04 that morning. I said *I love you* into the air and I started to sob and moan. I was alone, facing the first of many dark nights.

Chapter 41

Cremation

In the lower level of the Lakewood Cemetery Chapel is a crematorium. This is where Peter's body was taken to await cremation. I wanted to be there when he was cremated, even though some of my friends had voiced concern. I wanted to watch over him, to be in his presence, to accompany him until his body was transformed into ashes.

The room looked like a hospital operating room. Two kind men escorted me into this strange space, where I saw two gigantic furnaces set in a cement and brick wall. Another man, dressed in hospital scrubs, was rolling a gurney toward one of the furnaces. On it was a long, coffin-shaped box, made out of UPS brown, heavy corrugated cardboard. Inside the box was my dear husband. On the lid of the box was his name, handwritten: *Peter Y. Clark.* I reached out and touched the box. The three men in the room looked down, giving me a moment to say a silent goodbye to him. I leaned on the box, just as I had leaned on his body four days before in the hospital.

Then I stood back and the men slowly moved into action. The gurney had collapsible legs, like the ones in ambulances. One man was operating the furnace door, and the other two were aligning Peter's body box with the opening. Then, like choreography, the box rolled into the furnace, the door closed, and the sound of the burners took over the room.

I was silent for several minutes. And then I nodded to the men, quietly thanking them. I left the lower level of the chapel and stepped out into a stunningly beautiful day, bright sunshine in a cloudless blue sky.

Chapter 42

Three Days After Peter Died

I have never felt the presence of a dead person. Before January 21, 2012, I would have said that the dead do not communicate with the living — in my experience. My parents have been gone for many years, and I have neither felt their presence nor any message communicated by them. Despite two bizarre occurrences within 72 hours of Peter's death, I might still agree with myself. But they cause me to pause …

1. Peter died on a Saturday. By the following Tuesday morning, 11 light bulbs blew out in the house. Some were in lamps; some were recessed lights in the ceiling. Also, the battery in Peter's Prius was dead. Further, a streetlight near the front of our house started to flicker at night. Even the neighbors noticed it.

2. On Tuesday morning, I wanted to drive to the airport to pick up a friend. Many people at the house protested this idea saying, *No, no, Gail. Don't drive. It's too soon. You're distracted.* But I insisted that I needed to get in the car and do something normal. I went to the garage, where my car was parked next to the dead Prius. As I put the key in the ignition, I noticed something on the floor of the car. It was a piece of paper with something written on it. On top of the paper was a heart-shaped rock. I leaned over and picked it up. On the piece of paper, in Peter's handwriting it said: *I love you, Gail Hartman. Really.*

Chapter 43

The Death Certificate

Still reeling from Peter's death and carrying around a fatigue as thick as fog, I went to my front door to get the mail. It was stuffed with condolence cards, a bill or two in the mix. It was a week and a half after Peter's death. Embedded in the pile of mail was a large envelope containing 10 copies of Peter's death certificate. This legal document, stiff and formal in its appearance, would be necessary to prove his death to credit card and insurance companies, airlines, banks and the Social Security

Administration. I took them out of the envelope, impressed with the heavy, watermarked security paper. The print was in bold black letters, all caps. Each copy was bordered in a raised blue ink design with two embossed State Seals of Minnesota at the bottom.

After all that Peter went through, after all the suffering and complications, it all comes down to this one piece of paper, I thought. It was the coldest document I had ever seen. It made a mortgage deed look like a lyric poem. His name, Social Security number, birthdate and place of birth were listed in the first section. Then beneath were his date of death, where he died, his marital status, the name of his spouse, where he resided, his mother's and father's names, the name of the funeral home and his "Disposition," which was "CREMATION." It concluded with the cause of death: "HYPOXIC RESP FAILURE, BRADYCARDIA ARREST, PNEUMONIA, PULM FIBROSIS, SHORT TELOMERE SYNDROME."

Placing the copies back in the envelope, I climbed the stairs and entered my bedroom, which just 10 days ago had been our bedroom. I got under a blanket, wept for a while and fell asleep for the rest of the afternoon.

Chapter 44

The Mutation

Genetics: the gift that keeps on giving. In August of 2012, seven months after Peter died, his older brother, David, was winded after taking a two-mile walk. He went to the doctor and was given the dreaded diagnosis of IPF. His son, Bennett, an internist at Johns Hopkins, recommended that David come to Baltimore to be seen by a pulmonary specialist there. While David was there, unexpectedly his lung collapsed and following that by a few days, he had a major stroke and never regained consciousness. He died on September 21, 2012, eight months to the day from the date of Peter's death. David was 68. It seemed to me that no one took seriously the information Peter and I unearthed at the NIH until then. David's two children, Bennett and Gordon, got tested for the mutation because they were considering having children. Gordon has not inherited it, but sadly, Bennett at age 37, has. Subsequently, Bennett's two children were tested in utero. Fortunately, neither has inherited the pernicious mutation.

I have been told that Peter's sister has tested positively for the mutation, but is asymptomatic at age 73. His younger brother has chosen not to be tested, the same choice made by Alex and Emily. Alex has said that he plans to be tested when he is ready to have children. Since there is neither treatment nor cure for IPF, Emily has chosen never to find out if she has the mutation.

Chapter 45

The Eulogy

Peter's memorial service was held a month following his death. It took place in the main sanctuary of the First Unitarian Church, to which we did not belong. There were approximately 600 people in attendance. As these kinds of rituals go, it was extraordinarily meaningful and beautiful. I had spent the month planning it, with wonderful friends stepping forward to help me. The live music was outstanding, which felt important, since Peter loved music as much as he loved anything. And finally, the minister who conducted the service was as warm, sensitive and articulate as anyone I had ever met. Peter would have loved her.

Three scheduled eulogies were delivered. The first two were by close friends. I gave the third one. I wanted to speak for a couple of reasons: one, I needed our children to see that this terrible loss could be survived, and two, I felt an irrepressible urge to describe how Peter lived and how he died. I spoke for 25 minutes, not that I intended to. Here is what I said at the very end:

> *About two years ago, I was talking by phone to James Hollis, a Jungian analyst and writer — and an important mentor of mine. We were talking about illness and about death and loss. He told me something so simple and true: that everyone we love — be it a child, a parent, a friend, a sister or a brother — will either lose us or we will lose them. It's as simple as that. And so if being alive is in large part about loving, then being alive is also about loss and dying. Somehow this has been a great comfort to me. This ordeal of loving and losing and grieving is a part of being human — something we all have in common. Everyone in this room. My grief and sadness about losing Peter is there because I love him so much — which means that I am alive and am in awe of the whole difficult experience. The sadness I feel is no greater than the gratitude I have for sharing 37 years with such a remarkable person, whom I have loved and respected more than I can say.*

Chapter 46

Burying the Ashes

About a dozen friends joined Emily, Alex and me at Lakewood Cemetery on Monday, July 2, 2012. It was a sweltering day: 102 degrees with a dew point in the 80s. We gathered at the gravesite at 3:00. The cemetery had prepared the hole and had the concrete vault set up on what looked like a little stage for gnomes or elves. I had spray-painted the vault the same shade of blue as his 1953 Dodge pickup truck, so it did not look quite as funereal as it sounds. Someone read a Mary Oliver poem and another person read one by Wendell Berry. Most of Peter's ashes were in a beautiful stoneware urn, made by a friend of ours. I had removed some of the ashes so that the kids and I could spread them in our garden, at Lake Superior and in Lake Harriet.

When it was time to place the urn into the vault, many people stepped forward to place mementos, letters, tokens of affection inside of it to keep Peter company. Alex had brought a letter along with an organic avocado. (Peter believed that avocados are a perfect food.) Emily placed a letter and a tennis ball into the vault, our friend (who is also our financial advisor) put in two one-dollar bills honoring Peter's frugality, and another friend put in CDs of Joni Mitchell and Bob Dylan. I added a long letter, some pictures of our family, a small toy pickup truck and several smooth round stones from the North Shore. No doubt most of these treasures have disintegrated by now, transformed into a loving compost of sorts.

We watched the vault, filled with his ashes and gifts, being lowered into the ground. Then we went back to my house where we enjoyed air conditioning and Thai spring rolls, to honor Peter's last meal in the hospital the night before he died. Later that evening, Emily, Alex and I scattered some of his ashes in our garden. While we were at it, we also scattered the ashes of two of our beloved deceased cats and some of my mother's ashes from three years ago. I declared that I could not allow my house to remain a mausoleum, so on a warm, sultry evening, the three of us walked through Russian sage, zinnias, peonies, gigantic hosta, columbine and bee balm, scattering ashes, talking about love, the earth and life, as this long day was coming to an end.

Epilogue

It has been 16 years since Peter had the portacaval shunt liver surgery at the Mayo Clinic, nine years since he was diagnosed with idiopathic pulmonary fibrosis, and six years since the morning he died before my eyes in the Intensive Care Unit at Hennepin County Medical Center. My children and I have honored his birthday each year he has been gone by going to dinner at one of his favorite restaurants. We have visited him at the cemetery hundreds of time, leaving at his grave an assortment of tributes: cake doughnuts from a bakery he loved, many avocados, flowers from our garden and rocks of all kinds. There is bench not far from where his ashes are buried on the edge of the small, beautiful lake inside Lakewood. I have cried my eyes out on that bench. I have written poetry there, taken pictures of egrets, ducks and geese. I have seen eagles and hawks, fox and deer. I often walk in the cemetery, finding it to be the most peaceful place I know of in the city.

I talk to Peter sometimes, usually just in my head, but occasionally I have spoken out loud when I have pressing news for him. I went to his grave the day after the last presidential election and I wept as I told him about the shocking, disturbing results. The one good thing about being dead is that you are free from worry and despair. Peter missed the shooting of Trayvon Martin, the attacks in Benghazi, the mass shooting at Sandy Hook, the Boston Marathon bombings, the rise of ISIS, the suicide of Robin Williams, the Ebola epidemic, the *Charlie Hebdo* attack in Paris, the opioid epidemic, the European refugee crisis, the Zika virus, the Freddie Gray case, innumerable shootings, hurricanes, earthquakes and tornadoes. And he neither suffered the burden nor heartbreak of having Donald Trump in the White House. Of course he also missed some great things, like the reelection of Obama for a second term, the legalization of same sex marriage, and Bob Dylan receiving the Nobel Prize in Literature.

Alex and Emily lost their father too early in their lives, yet they have landed on their feet. Both of them now live in the Twin Cities, for which I'm grateful. Alex is now the owner of the 1953 Dodge pickup truck. Other than attending the wedding of one of my nieces in 2014, I have not seen Peter's sister or his surviving brother and their families. As I said, I am cut from a different cloth, and our relationship was defined by family rituals and a shared love of Peter. Now with Peter's parents gone, along with Peter and David, there is not enough tensile strength to hold us together. This is something I accept easily. Our nephew Bennett (David's oldest son, the one who has inherited the mutation), his wife and two small children have recently moved to Minneapolis. Having them here feels like our family has expanded in a wonderful way, and Alex, Emily and I are delighted.

I have used almost all of Peter's bricks in some new landscaping in the front yard. His cobblestones make a lovely border in the boulevard garden. And all the heart-shaped rocks we collected during our marriage are piled high on a terra cotta dish that is on the ground under a rose bush. His death books are neatly shelved in a bookcase in my bedroom.

My life is no longer organized around the constant management of fear. An intense drive to learn as much as I could about the liver, the lungs, the relationship between the two diseases was fueled by my fear of losing Peter, of becoming a widow, of our family changing, of being alone. And now I have lost him. I am a widow. Our family has changed and I'm alone, uncoupled, living in the same wonderful house I shared with him for so many years. I thought that these realities would be unbearable; I lay in bed in the dark so many nights over 10 years, terrified of what has now become my current life. I had no idea that I would not only survive those fears and dreads, but that I would also be thriving in the face of them. If people had told me this, I would not have believed them.

Grief is both excruciating and wondrous. It is the most painful of states, the agony and suffering that comes from losing someone you love. It ebbs and flows; it is an energy that is always inside you. In the beginning, I gave in to it. I had no choice. It wrestled me into bed, it overtook me when the sun both rose and set, it was a relentless force. And then eventually, after a couple of years, I got better and better at living with it, at taking it with me everywhere. Grief is rhythmic, like the tides — calm much of the time, and then without warning, a tsunami of sadness strikes. Grief has brought me to my knees. I would never have guessed that it would also propel me into a new life.

One day in August 2012, I was driving home from a long walk I had taken at the University of Minnesota Arboretum. It was a beautiful summer day, cottony cumulus clouds in a beautiful blue sky. I found it helpful to be outside in nature when the grief spells were rough. The strangest thing happened in the car as I was making my way home to my empty house. I had a thought — no, a knowing — that came from out of the blue: *I will be fine. I will be more than fine. I am entering a new life, one all my own, to create as I wish, to invent.* I could feel in my bones that I was shifting from a life oriented around negotiation, compromise, illness, caregiving to a life more self-defined, more autonomous, freer. I knew then that I would write, I would release myself from the habits of the past and create new channels in my life. I remember smiling as I realized that Peter's death would not define me forever, that the ordeal we went through would eventually be integrated inside me, resulting in greater depth and awareness. In the car, on that summer afternoon, I realized Peter's life was over, and that mine was not.

While losing Peter has been one of the most difficult events of my life — perhaps the most painful — it has made me a better therapist and it has allowed me to be a more creative person. I am no longer afraid of being alone, being a widow. Because of Peter's illness and death, I have a perspective about living and dying, about fear and survival, about the responsibility of living the most meaningful life possible. And while I am sadder, I have also become wiser. How can I be grateful for something as agonizing as loss and grief? Yet I am. I am also endlessly thankful that I got to spend 37 years of my life with someone I deeply loved and respected. Not everyone is this fortunate. As odd as this sounds, I feel like one lucky widow.

Social Security

Today is the day of my appointment at the Social Security Administration. I am carrying a file containing both my marriage license and my husband's death certificate. It had been difficult getting a certified copy of the marriage license. We married in California 35 years ago. I did not have a clue in which county our wedding had taken place. Many emails, notarized forms, proof of birth and citizenship, and a check for $60 later, I received a lovely document with swirled handwriting and an embossed emblem summarizing the details of that lovely day in May 1977.

The other certificate I am carrying is my husband's death certificate. I have many copies at home in a file marked "Death." A death certificate, if you've never seen one, is an ominous document with words that clinically reveal when and where a death took place, and then why and how the death occurred. It says that my dear husband (identified by name and Social Security number) was born in Palo Alto, California, on November 17, 1948. It goes on to say that he died on January 21, 2012, in Minneapolis, Minnesota, and that he was married to me, and it states the names of his parents. The funeral home is identified and the cremation is called his "disposition." The last section details the cause of death (hypoxic respiratory failure, bradycardia arrest, pneumonia, pulmonary fibrosis and short telomere syndrome). There are so many stories to tell about the life and death of my husband and the ordeal of his illnesses, but that's for another time.

On my way into the Social Security Administration building, I have to walk carefully, since the parking lot is not well plowed. The snow and ice are like barricades. I consider not parking the car and just skipping the whole experience. I am there to file for "death benefits." How can there be any benefit from this death? I don't want money, I want my husband back. I am doubting that the people at Social Security will be able to help with that.

I enter the building and am asked to put my purse on a counter so that a tall, young policeman can search it. And then he asks me to leave my keys and any metal jewelry in a receptacle while I walk through a metal detector, like the ones at airports. Once I'm on the other side, I am given my belongings and a number that I am supposed to keep until it is called over a loudspeaker. The waiting room is full of people. There is nowhere to sit. Many do not have coats. I am the only Caucasian in the room except for the policeman at the door. There are children running around, not seeming to be watched or cared for. There is another policeman near the counter where the numbers are being called. He is holding the leash of a large dog that I imagine is trained to smell drugs, guns and bombs. Did you know that there was so much security at Social Security? I did not.

I am feeling very self-conscious. I have a warm coat and a purse that has enough money in it. I think fairness is not at play here. Not anywhere, really. I smile at the children climbing on the dirty seats and they don't seem to notice me. I silently send them wishes of love and safety. *We're all in this together*, I say to myself. And then I hear my number called (so to speak). A young woman named Tranquilla greets me at Door 4. I think how ironic her name is, given the ambience of her workplace. She instructs me to go to stall 11 and she will meet me there. I am walking down a hall with stalls on either side. There are people yelling and translators helping with communication. Worn out wheelchairs litter the hall. I sit down in stall 11 and Tranquilla is already there, her computer turned on. She explains that she will be taping our interview. I have to sign something saying this is OK with me. I wonder what she would do if I refused to sign. I feel sure that has happened here before. Since I want to leave this place as soon as possible, I smile and am compliant. She asks me if I have my marriage license. I take out my file and give it to her. She types away at her computer. Now she wants to know if I have my husband's death certificate. She asks me if the dates are correct: *You got married on May 28, 1977? The date of your husband's death was January 21, 2012?* I think, *You've got to be kidding. It's all right there. Maybe she wants to rub it in. I know when I got married and I know my husband's dead. How many ways shall we discuss this?* She looks at her computer screen while I corroborate all the information on the certificates. As she enters the data of our lives, I decide to take out my phone and use the calculator to figure out how many days and hours we were married: 13,505 days, 324,120 hours.

He was my person, the love of my life, my partner till the moment he took his last, labored breath. I am remembering how he loved Friday nights together, the workweek done. I wish he would be home later so that I could tell him about my afternoon at the Social Security office. I can see the smile on his face. I know that he was aware of how much I would miss him. We had a long time to talk about the end and after the end. I wonder if Tranquilla would like to know what kind of a person he was and how much I loved him. I decide she would not be interested and I do not hold it against her. She deals with death and retirement, disability and Medicare, veterans benefits and government pensions. She is paid to not care about the stories.

We are at the end of our time together, Tranquilla and I. I thank her and she tells me that I will be getting a letter from Social Security before my next birthday, telling me how much money I will receive every month. I want to say: *Keep the damn money.* But then I remember how hard my husband worked and how much he loved what he did. Social Security will not bring him back, so the next best thing they can do is give you some money.

I pull out of the parking lot and feel a heaviness in my chest. It all comes down to this: forms, documents, proofs of birth, marriage and death. Who were you? Where were you from? When and where did you marry? When and how did you die? And here's some money for a survivor, reflecting your time working on earth. Social Security, I decide, is an oxymoron. I know it is a valuable part of our society and its future is in question. As I wait at a red light on my way home, I think about what other name would be better: The Security Center for the Living, The Bureau for Survivors, Benefits R Us.

I am thinking about Tranquilla. Does she go home this Friday night and tell her husband what she heard and recorded today? I hope they love each other. One of them will lose the other. There's no way out of that for any of us. She or her husband will end up in stall 11, confirming the facts of a life. And it will be tape-recorded. I hope for them it will be a long way off. I turn into my driveway at about 5:00 p.m., glad that this day is almost over. I enter my house and go to my desk. I put all the paperwork I acquired today into a file I label "Death Benefit," and then I lie down on my bed, or should I say on my side of our bed, and fall sleep, fully clothed, until morning.

Visitation at 35,000 Feet

I have been on 12 plane flights in the five years I have been a widow. My husband died in January of 2012 and in that time, I have been to Vancouver, New York, Baltimore twice, Amsterdam, Florence and now this flight to Boston for my nephew's law school graduation. I can't say I like to fly. It is a means to an end. I used to be afraid of flying, but in the last few years, it has been different. As I age, I am increasingly aware that I will actually die someday, that something will take me out. I would hate it to be a plane crash, but cancer is no afternoon at the beach either. These days, I bring a book and my iPad, on which I write poetry. Some of my best poems have been written up in the clouds.

My husband, whose name was Peter Clark, would have loved attending our nephew's graduation. He spent his career helping children and families negotiate school systems from preschool to college. He believed that all kids, even ones with learning problems, deserve a great experience in school — and he helped the struggling ones and their families. I felt a wave of sadness that neither was he here to attend this event, nor was he alive to see our two children go to graduate school several years ago. At the moment you lose someone you love, you gain a lifetime companion — grief. At first it has you in a stranglehold and later on, after you realize it is here for the duration of your time on earth, you get better at living beside it, with it, getting acclimated to its rhythms.

This trip I was taking to Boston was important. My nephew had lost his brother two months earlier, and this graduation was a much-needed celebratory event for our family. His grandmother was coming from Arizona, his mother's significant other was flying in from California, his father was driving north from Baltimore, and I was in flight from Minneapolis to Logan Airport. I had a small carry-on and a tote bag filled with the newspaper, *Commonwealth* by Ann Patchett, the current *New Yorker*, some sudoku puzzles, a baggie of nuts and raisins, and a bottle of water.

This was an early morning flight, leaving Minneapolis at 6:15 a.m. I figured it would not be crowded, but they announced at the gate that the flight was full. My seat was on an aisle, fairly close to the front of the plane. Once everyone was boarded and they closed the door of the aircraft, there was no one sitting in the middle seat between me and the woman by the window. She and I took advantage of this precious and unexpected space by placing our books and newspapers there. I was in row 10, seat D. Across the aisle, in seats A, B and C, there were three women, all squeezed in like marinated artichoke hearts. I was grateful for the empty middle seat next to me. The woman by the window in seat F (I will call her woman F) was busy getting settled as we heard the expected request to turn off our cell phones. She and I smiled at each other at some point, but we did not speak. I don't need to make friends on an airplane. My introverted self constructs an imaginary moat around my head. I give off no scent, no desire to get to know any new person. I'm not particularly proud of this, but I accept it.

When planes begin to speed down the runway and take off, I like to see what the passengers are doing. Some are asleep, avoiding the whole gravity-defying process. Others are chewing gum as though they are detoxing from a nicotine habit. Many of them are sitting, eyes open, with noise-canceling earphones on their heads. Maybe they are listening to a podcast or music. And there are always a few who are looking furtively at the wings, keeping their eyes on the screws and bolts holding the engines in place. I used to be in this last category. Now I am just an interested observer, sublimating the remaining shards of fear into useless sociological surveys.

It was a blessedly smooth flight once we got to the cruising altitude of 35,000 feet. The pilot turned off the seat belt sign and people began to get up to use the bathroom. For the first hour of the flight, I read the paper and *The New Yorker*. Woman F asked if she could read the first two sections of the paper now that it was just lying in the empty seat between us. I said, *Sure, it's all yours.* Then, lest she think I might want to chat, I got my book out and starting reading.

In another half hour, woman F leaned forward to get something out from under the seat in front of her. She seemed to be having a hard time reaching whatever she was looking for, so she turned her head toward the aisle to achieve a better stretch. I was trying not to let on that I was watching this maneuver. She then recognized a woman sitting directly across the aisle from me in seat C (let's call her woman C).

Woman F said loudly, *Hi! I can't believe it's you! And we're on the same ridiculously early flight!*

Oh my God, what a coincidence! woman C replied, looking happily surprised.

Woman F was clearly glad to have someone to talk to. I pretended I was reading *Commonwealth* and turned the pages at a rate that seemed plausible for a reader. But in fact, I was eavesdropping. I found out that woman F was an orthopedist, in the middle of an acrimonious divorce. She had three children, ages nine to fifteen, and two of them were sitting somewhere at the rear of the plane. The third was a boy, Ned, and he was "on the spectrum." She and her almost-ex-husband sent him to a boarding school in New Hampshire. In fact, that is where she and her other two children were going — to Ned's ninth-grade graduation. They were going to rent a car at Logan and head straight to New Hampshire.

It seemed that woman C knew woman F's family well. She asked all kinds of questions and seemed particularly interested in how Ned was doing. She mentioned that she was going to meet her daughter and son-in-law in Boston and help them move to Maine over the weekend. She said her husband, quite a bit older than she, did not have the stamina to help with the move. I kept turning the pages of my book, invisible to them. Woman F asked woman C if she thought about retiring. I was guessing that woman C was also a physician. They talked about burnout and wanting to avoid it — and they spoke of the pluses and minuses of working part time.

After about 20 minutes of talking, woman F let out a big sigh, as she was talking again about Ned. She said to woman C, *You know who I would give anything to talk to? Just for an hour? Peter Clark. I miss Peter Clark.*

I think I stopped breathing for a minute. Peter Clark, my husband, dead five and a half years.

She went on: *He helped us more than anyone with Ned. He really understood children like no one else. The school is not the same without him.*

I was incredulous. I forgot to turn the page in the book. My face was suddenly warm.

Oh, I can't believe you are mentioning Peter! said woman C. *I was just telling my husband on the way to the airport this morning how much I wish I could talk to Peter about so many of the kids I work with. No one knew kids like he did. I really miss him.*

And then without skipping a beat, I came out from under my shroud of invisibility and said, *I miss him, too.*

They were stunned. I even heard woman F gasp. Woman C said: *Did you know Peter?*

And I said proudly, *He was my husband.*

This was about the most enjoyable thing that had happened in my life in months. It was pure joy to see their shocked expressions.

Oh my God, are you Gail? said woman C.

I am! And who are you? She told me her name and we both laughed. She was Peter's favorite neuropsych testing person. He respected her enormously and referred everyone who needed testing to her. The pieces started falling into place. Woman F and her family, especially Ned perhaps, had been helped by Peter, and he, no doubt, must have sent Ned to woman C for testing. The family sounded as though it had been living on the edge of chaos for some time. I suppose with three children how could it be otherwise?

Woman F told us several stories about Peter and how he helped her family. No one had been able to understand Ned's learning and social issues until they met Peter. Woman C asked how I was doing without Peter and how our kids were faring. I filled her in on the last five years and even showed them pictures on my phone of our children (now adults) and some of Peter long ago. Woman C knew a lot about our life — and even more about his illnesses. So for another half hour, at 35,000 feet, the three of us talked about Peter Clark, the colleague, the child advocate, the life partner.

When the plane landed in Boston, we parted ways, wishing one another a good time on the East Coast. As I was walking to the taxi stand outside the airport, I remembered that Peter told a story about being at the Sistine Chapel on a post-college trip to Europe. He was looking up at the ceiling and from somewhere behind him, he heard a voice: *Hey, Clark!* It was an old friend from Palo Alto High School in California. What is the likelihood of running into someone you know at the Sistine Chapel? Well, I think this airplane occurrence tops the Sistine Chapel event. It was like the lottery odds: to be seated on an airplane at 6:15 in the morning, between two people who just happened to know each other and who both knew and missed my deceased husband.

I don't know that I have ever felt Peter's presence the way some people describe experiences with the dead. I certainly think about him all the time. And the grief, the longing to talk to him, to hear his voice, to be with him happens frequently. But I could swear that he had something to do with this Minneapolis to Boston flight. Was that seat between woman F and me really empty? The flight attendant said that it was a sold-out flight. Did Peter choreograph this meeting in the sky? I loved showing pictures of him to my traveling companions, and hearing their stories brought him to life again. It was like three-part harmony:

I miss Peter Clark.

I really miss Peter.

I miss him, too.

For all anyone knows, he wanted me to have company way above the earth, in a silver projectile going 500 miles per hour. Maybe this was Peter's doing, an activity in the afterlife. Taking the middle seat. Creating synchronicity. Visiting me on my way to Boston.

Haiku

∾

three women who write
sit, in the heat of summer,
wowing each other

Roget's Thesaurus:
most generous book ever,
giving away words

to think of a book,
May 4th, 2018,
a gift to myself

it comes out of me,
sometimes the timing is right:
words, letters, writing

working on haiku:
little poems, like dessert,
perfectly portioned

∾

I've had many lives
within these 70 years;
each one, a chapter

the older I get
the more I detest shopping
stores: little cages

the nutritionist
looked unhappy; maybe she's
tired of food groups

live, love, lose — repeat
over and over till death;
I am sure of this

elasticity:
that's what we lose as we age,
we're old rubber bands

~

toddlers are outraged;
they can't get over the truth:
they are not in charge

constant adjustments:
attitudes, thoughts, body, moods
staying vertical

the wisest advice:
do not compete with yourself
when you were younger

here's what I don't like:
absence of warmth, arrogance
the way people leave

in the morning sky:
white waning moon winks at me,
my friend since childhood

꩜

Lillian Hellman:
the figure in my childhood
sleeping beneath me

New Yorker picture:
Rachel Maddow relaxing;
I want a girlfriend

thinking of changing,
turning myself upside down
my life, a snow globe

I'm still inside me,
good thing to check now and then:
the soul's fire drill

a window opens
memories come flooding in;
glad I've had a life

∾

"hold on to yourself"
I say over and over,
my East Coast mantra

my mother lived life
telling us and herself lies:
no wonder she cracked

writing down the facts
an enigma, my mother:
so many secrets

cautionary tales:
their lives teach by example,
mother and father

love is like water,
necessary for living,
and both can be scarce

∽

inside my own brain
there's a secret government
calling all the shots

amazed ev'ryday:
my life is in the Midwest,
so much gratitude

homeostasis:
do things really ever change
or just switch places?

some sacred secrets
stored in my body's attic,
best kept tucked away

curiosity:
it killed the cat, but not me,
at least not so far

ℬ

"I am so lonely,"
she laid her head down and cried,
left her secret here

long days of patients:
ev'ryone is scared of death,
what a line of work

throwing away gold:
telling a person the truth
while they're not list'ning

all the disorders
are about love gone awry:
too much, not enough

being dutiful
is such an emergency:
the soul is silenced

∾

shame, like a bad smell,
gets worse until you think to
open the window

when does solitude
make that sharp turn, ending up
as isolation?

magical other:
someone who will make you whole,
a nice fairy tale

aware of missing
something that will not happen:
a strange nostalgia

sanctimonious,
Holy Roller happiness:
a warped point of view

⁓

the authors would know:
Adela, a lonely child,
such a good story

a girl from New York,
a girl from Minnesota
create a French tale

love, a mystery
a common thread, like water
essential for life

a story finished,
glad and sad at the same time,
a gain and a loss

Rilke late at night:
the words tuck me in, my brain
soothed, loved before sleep

～

I love begonias,
the tuberous kind that droop:
stunning old women

mallards in my yard,
two of them reading the *Times*,
bored with migration

birds at the feeder
all immigrants of a kind;
each one is welcome

well, it's white again
outside, snow covers green grass,
goodbye to sidewalks

tomorrow morning's
wind chill, 21 below:
winter's showing off

～

wouldn't you know it:
pulmonary fibrosis
fits in a haiku

illness took over
we had no choice but to deal:
now I tell the tale

fear entered our house
the day he had an X-ray,
his lungs: death sentence

writing it all down,
the decline of a loved one,
what was I thinking?

blue oxygen tanks
covered with warnings: danger
they lived in our house

∾

grief: it makes itself
at home whenever it wants;
we have no control

when I was afraid
I learned about gratitude:
lovely antidote

memory appears:
his scar wrapped around his chest
just like a zipper

widowed oracle:
a role I neither wanted
nor auditioned for

if he were alive
he would have been 69
today, his birthday

nightly bedfellows:
sadness, gratitude and fear;
sleep settles them down

alone, solo, seule
one, unit, single, widow
unaccompanied

the doctor explains:
lens gets cloudy, years of use
like old window glass

the blue pickup truck
summer spins around the lake
feeling safe from harm

the cemetery,
always peaceful and quiet,
dead people don't talk

the house is filled up
carbohydrates ev'rywhere
this must be shiva

living all alone:
smaller loads in the washer,
more room in the bed

an apparition:
I thought I saw him again,
feeling my heart break

obituaries:
reading them every day
tiny short stories

ev'ryone went home;
alone again in this house
deep breath, start again

The text of *Preserving Light* is set in Adobe Minion Pro, a typeface designed by Robert Slimbach in 1990 for Adobe Systems and inspired by late Renaissance-era type. An OpenType update of the original family was released in 2000. The titles are set in Cochin, a typeface originally produced in 1912 by Georges Peignot for the Paris foundry G. Peignot et Fils and based on the copperplate engravings of French 18th-century artist Charles-Nicolas Cochin. This book was designed by Patti Frazee and Gail Hartman. The book was edited by Stevie Beck; the cover was designed and photographed by Janet Mills. Manufactured by Ingram.